mindful knitting

mindful knitting

INVITING CONTEMPLATIVE PRACTICE TO THE CRAFT

Tara Jon Manning

TUTTLE PUBLISHING

Boston · Rutland, Vermont · Tokyo

First published in 2004 by Tuttle Publishing, an imprint of Periplus Editions (HK) Ltd., with editorial offices at 153 Milk Street, Boston, Massachusetts 02109.

ISBN: 0-8048-3543-8
Library of Congress Control Number: 2004103646

Distributed by

NORTH AMERICA,
LATIN AMERICA & EUROPE
Tuttle Publishing
Distribution Center
Airport Industrial Park
364 Innovation Drive
North Clarendon, VT 05759-9436
Tel: (802) 773-8930
Fax: (802) 773-6993
info@tuttlepublishing.com
www.tuttlepublishing.com

JAPAN
Tuttle Publishing
Yaekari Building, 3rd Floor
5-4-12 Ōsaki
Shinagawa-ku
Tokyo 141 0032
Tel: (03) 5437-0171
Fax: (03) 5437-0755
tuttle-sales@gol.com

ASIA PACIFIC
Berkeley Books Pte. Ltd.
130 Joo Seng Road
#06-01/03 Olivine Building
Singapore 368357
Tel: (65) 6280-1330
Fax: (65) 6280-6290
inquiries@periplus.com.sg

First edition
08 07 06 05 04   10 9 8 7 6 5 4 3 2 1

Photography by Bill Manning • Photo styling by Tara Jon Manning
Technical edits by Lori Gayle • Design by Gopa & Ted2, Inc.

Printed in Canada

acknowledgments

THANKS TO THE VERABLE CHÖGYAM TRUNGPA RINPOCHE for manifesting the vision, and to the Sakyong Mipham Rinpoche and Shambhala International for holding and moving it forward into the twenty-first century.

Thanks to Ane Pema Chödrön for saying it all in a way that everyone can understand.

Thanks to my parents for following their path to the Dharma and bringing me with them.

Thanks to Bill, Jack, and Zane for constantly renewing my understanding of the depths of true love.

Thanks to Joan Anderson for her insight, support, and foudroyance.

Thanks to Linda Roghaar and the Linda Roghaar Literary Agency for seeing the delight in the idea, unending support and encouragement.

Thanks to Jennifer Lantagne and Tuttle Publishing, Lori Gayle, Lynn Gates, the manufacturers and distributors who graciously supplied the materials, and to all the knitters who know the essence of mindfulness found on the needles.

contents

part one: becoming a mindful knitter

chapter one

chapter two

chapter three

part two: more mindful knitting projects

preface

dharma brat, dharma knitter

IN SOME WAYS I don't remember when mindfulness, meditation, and Buddhism were not a part of my life. When I was a child, my parents moved to Boulder, Colorado, to study with a Tibetan Rinpoche (a Tibetan Buddhist teacher) named Chögyam Trungpa. And as a child, I came to view the seemingly mystical and exotic world of meditation, Tibetan rituals, monks in burgundy robes, and people with names such as Vajra and Padma as totally normal. As my parents became students of the dharma (the teachings of the Buddha), the dharma became the roadmap for my world, and I grew up within the first wave of what has affectionately come to be known as dharma brats. As I now come into my own adulthood, I have begun to understand more fully the power of the things that I have experienced and have been taught. As a kid it was just the way it was, although I knew I was more than just a little different from the average teenager. But as I explore my own relationship with meditation practice and the preciousness of experience, I am coming to realize more profoundly the great fortune of my view of the world and the very unique gifts of mindfulness and awareness.

My life as a knitter is also one whose origins are hard to pinpoint. My mom knit many sweaters for me when I was a child. She always invited me to participate in their design and creation. I would help her decide where to embroider little flowers, or sew on groovy peace sign and rainbow patches. I remember wearing my little cardigans and hooded pullovers with pride. She claims I would sit for hours watching her knit until the sweaters were ready to wear. I learned to knit around age eight, with what I'm sure was the first of many unfinished projects. I remember starting a lot of scarves but never completing them. I began making mittens around age nine, and still get grief over the fact that our house was purportedly full of left mittens, since my attention would wander and I'd never make the matching right. It was here that I embarked on a career as a "chronic starter," continually seduced by a new color or a fresh stripe sequence. As a young child, I found knitting and handwork in general to be an engaging way to pass the time, sewing and knitting wardrobes for dolls and teddy bears. As a teenager, I learned of the soothing and stress relieving aspects of knitting and finished my first sweater in high school. I became voracious about trying out new things—socks, colorwork, intarsia. I would just see something that looked fun and try it. I knew I had something when my mom began to ask me for knitting help.

In college I began to study fine arts and explore world textile traditions. I continued to knit furiously, often getting weird looks from other students. I began bringing my knitting to art history lectures, and within a few weeks I was joined by two or three other knitters in the back of the room. Thus was I was introduced to the social aspect of knitting—the camaraderie and the joy of sharing.

After graduating from college, I was inspired to begin designing garments, and started designing kids' sweaters. This led me to a graduate program in apparel and textile design. My heart, however, could not be separated from my knitting, and I developed my own curriculum combining historical costume, fiber arts, and garment design, leading to a unique combination for a thesis topic. This whet my appetite for design and my passion for knitting was irreversible. I knit every day; in fact, I found that if I did not knit, I felt restless and edgy. I began to teach knitting classes, and to publish my sweater designs in knitting magazines. I wanted to connect more and more with the traditions of knitting and the community of knitters past and present. I found that knitting was grounding and fulfilling, and it provided me with a temporal connection with the women who came before me, as well as the events of my daily life.

contemplative knitting

As I continued to explore my own relationship with meditation practice, I was drawn more and more to the area of contemplative arts. My studies in art led me to explore the relationship between the work of the hands and the qualities of the mind. As my studies in art and my passion for knitting and textiles continued on a parallel course, I wondered more and more about the focused quality of mind elicited by knitting. In 1999 I opened a little knitting shop called Over the Moon in Longmont, Colorado, and often discussed this with my knitting friends and customers. As I began to practice meditation more, I also began to knit more, producing designs for publication or samples for the shop. In these knitting sessions, which typically lasted from two to four hours, I began to tune in to the commonalties between practicing mindfulness meditation and the actions of knitting. Both require light attention to the environment, both allow the mind to rest, both have a natural object of focus that contributes a rhythmic quality to the experience. I found that as I sat knitting in random places—a restaurant or a park—women young and old would approach me and ask what I was working on. Almost before I could answer they would launch into their own testimonials on the relaxing, calming qualities of knitting. They would offer stories of how a project transformed their lives, or how knitting provided them with a sense of safety during a hardship. I knew I was onto something, and I was not onto it alone.

What I have been exploring, and what I hope to impart to you, is the basic wakefulness available to anyone through engaging in daily mindfulness. By simply creating a quiet state of being, you can begin to notice—notice your thoughts, notice your feelings, and notice the workings of your mind and experience. Through this process of noticing we can begin to develop a kindness—toward ourselves and our world.

introduction

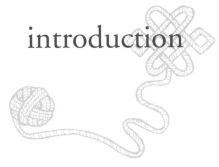

THE ACT OF KNITTING is inherently built on the formation of a stitch, the creation of fabric. When we knit, we place our attention over and over again on the natural rhythm of creating fabric from yarn—insert needle, wrap yarn, pull through a new stitch, repeat. Following this simple repetitive action is the basis of contemplative practice. It continually reminds us to stay focused, to stay in the moment. When we knit with this attention, we have an almost indescribable feeling of satisfaction and contentment. This is knitting as meditation.

As knitters, we know this soothing effect of our craft. When we knit, we dwell in our safe place—a quiet, focused, contemplative space. The ordinariness of the world gives way to a sense that every thing holds a little bit of magic. As we start to pay attention, we see that there's really a lot of magic around us. We recognize this magic, for example, in the feeling we experience when the amazing blue of the sky takes our breath away. We can give ourselves this gift of viewing everything with this sense of wonder and appreciation when we simply learn to focus our attention and notice ourselves and the world around us. In this spirit of cultivating a sense of wonder and magic through focused attention, I ask you to look at yourself as a "Mindful Knitter"—someone with an appreciation and awareness of the art of knitting.

This book presents knitting as a method for developing mindful focus. The exploration of how to use the relationship between yourself, your focus, and your handwork invites you to develop your own innate wisdom for relating directly—mindfully—to yourself and your experiences. Working through the themes and projects in each chapter, you will journey through the process of developing as a mindful knitter. Whether you are an advanced or a beginning knitter, a new or seasoned meditator, as you enrich your skills, your awareness of contemplative focus, and your solid place in the present moment, you can develop a unique and personal understanding of mindfulness in your relationship with your knitting. You already have a sense of that magical engagement with your craft. The essays and projects in this book will enable you to further discover your connection with your practice of knitting and your understanding of mindfulness, and will help you befriend yourself, the world, and everyone in it.

In part one, "Becoming a Mindful Knitter," a series of essays and practical knitting exercises will guide you on a path that begins with an introduction to basic meditation technique and how to use knitting as a mindfulness activity. You may thus start on the inside, accessing your own innate ability to be still and confidant, then gently move out into your immediate world, where you are asked to see the magic inherent in everything. As your own sense of dignity and awakening is encouraged through engaging with your craft, you will begin to see the effect that your state of mind and actions have on the bigger world. While you explore this through the filter of your opening heart, you are asked to explore how you and your simple actions— even your knitting—can contribute to the betterment of the bigger picture. Next, you are challenged to continue along the path of exploration, pushing your knitting skill and your commitment to engage in the world with purpose and mindfulness. I sincerely hope that this exploration of mindful knitting is only the beginning of your engagement with a mindful and compassionate life. All of this while you are knitting!

The projects in this book are delightful, fun to knit, and accessible to all knitters. Each one has been developed around a specific theme of mindfulness. The theme and the knitting complexity of the projects are presented in a graduated format. For the new knitter, beginning with the first project will engage you in building your knitting skills step by step, starting with a basic garter stitch project and leading up to an easy sweater. For the more advanced knitter, your intimate familiarity with knitting technique will allow you to explore more fully the mindfulness component of each exercise. Accompanying the projects are explanations of techniques and tips for easier or more intuitive knitting, assuring something of interest for everyone. Part two, "More Mindful Knitting Projects," presents five additional theme-specific original design projects developed to encourage you to look at everything you knit, and everything you do, as holding the opportunity to bring a mindful focus to your life.

As you complete the process of unfolding as a mindful knitter, consider keeping a companion journal where you can record your thoughts, frustrations, insights, and projects. Make note of when and where you were knitting, what materials you used, whom you were knitting for, and what insights working through the project brought you. Start a mindful knitting group and share these insights with other mindful knitters as you support one another on the journey. To further enrich your knitting experience, consider some of the outreach options presented by this book and its projects. Perhaps these exercises and projects built around the notion of knitting something to give away will inspire you to found a charity-knitting group, providing you a practical and enriching way to do something for the world.

The path of exploration of our minds and lives is very individual and unique, yet we are blessed to be on this journey with fellow travelers. As we explore mindfulness meditation and the working of our emotions and our minds, it is surprising to find amazing similarities in our experience. I hope that as you embark on your journey, you will strengthen your connection not only with yourself and your craft, but also with the lineage of other knitters in your community, your connection with your own precious heart, and the basic goodness inherent in all beings.

part one

BECOMING A MINDFUL KNITTER

chapter one
MEDITATION AND MINDFULNESS

HOW DOES ONE BEGIN to be mindful? Can being mindful really affect how we perceive the world? Absolutely! Mindfulness simply means engaging in what is happening from moment-to-moment, allowing ourselves to be aware of what is occurring in our minds and in our surroundings without judgment or interpretation—simply as an onlooker. As we purposefully elicit a state of mindful awareness, we begin to experience a peaceful, balanced state. In cultivating this preciousness in our experience, we become more and more anchored in our body and in the present moment, fostering a clear and calm state of being. Practicing mindfulness gives us the opportunity to develop a renewed and kind sense of who we are, naturally encouraging our self-confidence to grow.

Contemplative or "mindful" activities are any that allow us to practice mindfulness. These activities provide the circumstances for our minds to rest in the present. For some people this may be an activity such as prayer, for others it is gardening, yoga, or meditation. All these activities have a very important component in common—an object of focus that empowers us to retreat from our thoughts and feelings back to the sanctuary of our still and relaxed place. The object of focus for the simple mindfulness meditation instruction given in this book is the natural flow of breath. The object of focus for the mindful knitter is the repeated formation of the knitted stitch.

basic mindfulness meditation

The mindfulness activities and mindfulness meditation presented in this book are based on my experience of Tibetan Buddhism and the teachings of Chögyam Trungpa Rinpoche (1939–1987) and his eldest son, Sakyong Mipham Rinpoche. Trungpa Rinpoche, an esteemed meditation master and teacher in the traditions of the Kagyü and Nyingma lineages of Tibetan Buddhism, was elemental in bringing the teachings of Buddhism to Western students. Sakyong Mipham Rinpoche is head of the Shambhala Buddhist lineage and spiritual director of Shambhala International. Among the principles embraced by Shambhala Buddhism are the notions of innate human wisdom and basic goodness. The understanding and experience of these principles are deepened through the practice of mindfulness meditation.

The very basic form of mediation presented here involves the technique of sitting still in an upright posture and using the tool of focusing one's attention on the flow of breath. This technique is based on the basic sitting meditation instruction known in Shambhala Buddhism as Shamatha. It is a very elemental form of being still, making friends with yourself, and connecting with the richness available in your basic experience. It's also the core technique taught in the Shambhala Training program. Formal instruction in mindfulness meditation in the Shambhala tradition places a good deal of emphasis on the quality of discipline in the form. What this means is that you are encouraged to take this seriously. Keep your posture tall, hold your focus, and feel the connection with your innate dignity that begins to arise.

This form of basic mindfulness meditation can be done by anyone, anywhere, anytime, with no special supplies or gadgets. It does not ask anyone to relinquish any belief or buy into new ones; rather it allows you to explore the beliefs you hold close and engage more precisely in the world around you.

The first component of this meditation is creating a place—within yourself, within your day, within your life—where you can simply be still and quiet. Traditionally, a special place is designated for sitting meditation. You are encouraged to designate a clean, comfortable spot away from distraction where you can relax. In Buddhist and Shambhala traditions, a shrine or altar is placed in this space, not as something to worship or pray to but as a reminder to uplift your state of mind and experience. It often holds objects or photographs that inspire you. A little shrine in your meditation area can be anything you want it to be. It might simply be a little table with a candle and some flowers, or it could hold a photograph of a landscape or an individual important to you. I simply light a candle and burn some subtle incense when I engage in sitting mediation. The ritual of lighting the candle brings me a sense of presence and attention to the activity in which I am about to engage. It also nicely demarcates the beginning and end of my mediation session, allowing my focus to transition more easily from daily activity to my own quiet time, and back again.

Attention to your posture in meditation is very important. The traditional posture for meditation is to sit on the "ground" with your legs crossed, your back straight and your gaze loosely resting in front of you. When you sit on the ground or floor, you are literally "grounded." As you hold your back straight, you are extending your awareness both downward to the earth and upward to heaven, symbolically connecting the two and assuming your place in the world. This upright posture encourages your mind to be fully present in your body. Meditators often use meditation cushions, called *zabutons* and *zafus*. The zabuton is a rectangular flat cushion about thirty-six inches square. Upon the zabuton sits the zafu, a round cushion upon which one sits cross-legged. Many seats and cushions in all shapes, variations, and sizes are available, and you can try out different forms of cushions and seating. However, no special seating is actually required. You can practice this basic form of meditation while sitting in a chair, on the couch, or even lying down if necessary. Having reminders of why you are doing this around you is helpful, but having the right attitude is all you really need to get started.

Clearing out a quiet moment for yourself to try this basic technique in the midst of your daily routine can be wonderfully soothing. If you try to meditate when you are feeling antsy or slouchy, you may find that your mind is just too revved up and you may fight against yourself. That might simply not be the right time to try. Instead, keep your very important date with yourself by taking a walk or simply enjoying some quiet time with a cup of tea. In contrast, you may find that when everything is coming together, you have a session where your mind and body are feeling in synch. You are able to hold your posture and your focus and you may notice a natural equilibrium that begins to come through. Neither of these experiences is good or bad. Please remember to be kind and gentle with yourself. What is most important is that you keep with it; don't judge your experiences, but simply notice them and allow them to contrast one against another. The more you do this, the more you will find that you can be increasingly gentle with yourself. You may find clarity in situations that may have previously been confusing or scary.

After you have had a few practice sessions, you may discover that your thoughts assume a certain quality or theme during a particular session. Notice whether your mind and body seem to be existing in the same space, and notice when your mind wishes to be anywhere but here. Every session is different, none good, none bad, but all contribute to the development of a clearer quality of mind and a friendliness toward yourself.

The basic meditation instruction given in this chapter will become the foundation for using your knitting as a form of mindfulness practice. Try a combination of sitting meditation and mindful knitting throughout your week and allow the themes that will be explored in this book to encourage you to unfold. Try to establish a regular routine of mindfulness practice wherein you dedicate at least twenty minutes a day to cultivating this in your life. It could be in the mornings before your day begins, it could be over your lunch hour, or you could decide to switch off the TV or record your favorite shows and practice at the end of your day instead. Whatever works best for you, stick with it, and don't beat yourself up if you miss a day or two; just get back to it when you can.

1. *Set a time and place.* Look at your schedule and find a span of time in your day that you can mark off in your calendar and dedicate to yourself. Twenty minutes to half an hour is a great place to start. Allow yourself to be uninterrupted, and consider asking your family or household to support you in this. So that you are not distracted by the time, set a gentle alarm or ask someone to act as your timekeeper and knock on your door after twenty minutes. Your meditation space could be in a room alone, in the corner of your bedroom, in the garden—wherever it is, consider dedicating the spot to this activity as you continue to practice.

mindfulness instructions for basic meditation

2. *Establish your posture.* As discussed, your posture and the position of your body directly relate to and affect your state of mind. "Taking your seat" and assuming a proper posture is

elemental to cultivating the right attitude and encouraging a good experience. If you feel slouchy, you'll notice the difference. Your body will ache, your mind will be distracted, and often the quality of your experience is challenged. Find just the right place to sit within your chosen environment. As mentioned, a chair works fine, but make sure the chair allows you to sit upright with your feet firmly flat on the floor. This will emulate the grounded quality inherent in the traditional cross-legged posture. As you find the right level of sitting up straight, consider the adage "not too tight, not too loose." The right posture will be not too far forward, not too far back; you'll know it when you find it. It is said if you lean too far back, you are putting yourself in the past, and too far forward pushes into you the future. The perfect middle point in your posture allows you to be right here, right now. If you choose to sit cross-legged, take your position firmly on a soft surface or on your cushion. Using a pillow or cushion to raise your bottom off the floor will keep your legs from falling asleep too quickly. Once you have balanced these elements and find yourself feeling comfortable, just spend a few moments relaxing your body and calming your mind, bringing your attention to your experience. Keep your eyes open and allow your gaze to gently fall to the floor in front of you. You'll find the right spot—usually between four and six feet in front of you. Let your focus go soft so you are maintaining contact with your surroundings, but not focusing on any one thing. Doing this further maintains your connection with the experience of your body and discourages the mind from wandering—and keeps you from falling asleep!

3. *Find your breath.* This may sound a little obvious, but try it. Once you have relaxed into your posture and your environment, place your attention on the in-and-out flow of your breath. At first you will notice that you are breathing. Bring your breath in through your nose and lightly out through your mouth. After a bit you will naturally start to identify "in breath" and "out breath." Keep your attention lightly on this flow since the soft constancy of breathing provides a wonderful organic object of focus.

4. *Guide your attention back to your breath.* As you engage in watching the flow of breath, you will find that your attention has most likely wandered. It really doesn't matter where or why, but rather that you notice. When you make this observation, gently say to yourself "I'm thinking," or identify the thought as "thinking." Don't worry about what the thought was about. Don't try to trace its origin or destination, and most importantly, don't criticize

yourself for letting your mind wander. This is what minds do. Rather, return to the flow of your breath—until next time, and once again, when you notice you are involved in a conversation with someone who is not in the room, label it as "thinking" and bring your attention lightly back to your breath.

5. *Maintain your attention on the object of focus.* As you sit, continue to use the technique of following the breath, and gently recognizing and labeling your thoughts. Continue in this way for the duration of the time you have dedicated to your meditation.

Use these instructions as a starting point to explore your relationship with your daily routine and with yourself. Clear your mind before you start your day with a little open space by sitting quietly for ten minutes in the morning. Consider starting your mindful knitting sessions with a few minutes of simple quiet focus using the basic technique presented here.

To more fully explore formal meditation and benefit from it in the best possible way, individual meditation instruction is essential. Perhaps after working through this book or engaging in a regular meditation routine for a few weeks, you may choose to seek instruction and support for your practice. Many variations on mindfulness meditation are available. Consider speaking with someone at your place of worship or community center to discover variations on meditation techniques and find one that best suits you. One-on-one instruction can also be found through a study group or Shambhala center. Having a trained meditation instructor or meditation group led by a senior student or councilor will allow you to discuss your own experiences, understand the experiences of others, and have someone of whom you can ask questions when they arise.

chapter two

WHEN WE MEDITATE, we give ourselves a gift of time and a bit of open space in our day. The world eases off a little bit, and we create a safe and quiet place where we can just be, temporarily removed from the demands of deadlines, chores, and appointments. When we meditate, we find that simple and quiet place by deliberately creating it.

When we knit, we also find this still and quiet place. We often enter it when we sit down for a few minutes with our needles. Sometimes we may accompany it with a cup of tea, or for the more hardcore knitters, it may occur while we are stuck in a traffic jam. It can be anywhere, anytime. We enter into it by purposefully engaging in a focused activity. Our attention is specific to what is happening right there in our hands as the thoughts float away and our burdens are lifted. We can relax; we can enjoy ourselves. We recall a funny thing that happened during the day, or we can work out frustration, or dispel anger. We can also choose to simply be there, feeling the yarn move through our hands, hearing the sounds around us, and relishing the experience.

finding our focus

In meditation, our tool for creating this space is our focus on the natural flow of breath. In knitting, our focus is on the repeated formation of a stitch. When we use this focus in our knitting it gives us the opportunity to notice what's going on—to be mindful.

When we knit we make ourselves still and begin to work the yarn with the needles. At first we pay attention to setting up the row properly, to the directions in the pattern, to the feeling of a new yarn. Then, after a few stitches we're off—planning our trip for the weekend, trying to remember what we needed from the grocery store—and then we remember, "I think I was supposed to purl that stitch," and we're back, sometimes with a mistake as a permanent record of where our minds wandered off. When we stay focused on what's happening now, we relate directly with the pattern directions, the motion of our hands, the tactile feelings of the yarn, and we are in the moment. We are knitting with a contemplative focus: we are mindful knitters. We have connected with how knitting allows us a fresh breeze of spaciousness in our day, that little gift to ourselves.

Maintaining this focus can be difficult. Sometimes we are here, noticing the sounds around us—a car driving by, the neighbor's dogs barking. Then all of a sudden we're thinking about the phone call we forgot to return yesterday, our hearts start to race, and we remember: that's not happening now ("I'm thinking") and we're back to our body sensations. Before we know it, we're planning our kid's Halloween costume. After deciding how many layers he'll have to wear under it to stay warm, we remember "thinking" and we're again back to our hands and the yarn wrapping around the needle.

Instinctively use the sounds around you, the feeling of the yarn, the way the chair in which you are sitting feels, to bring you back to what is literally at hand. This focus can then expand to include awareness of the project you are creating, the connection you may feel toward the person for whom you are knitting, and the sensations that arise from that connection. The entirety of the situation brings you to a place that feels balanced, where your actions are deliberate, your intention is purposeful, and your world is a safe and spacious place.

As we begin to apply the concept of mindful activity to knitting, we begin to see that it can provide us with a precious gift—the ability to transform a mindless activity into a mindful activity. Making the choice to deliberately focus is a discipline, but so was learning to knit— and learning to walk, and learning to drive. As you continue to knit mindfully, you will begin to realize many of the benefits that arise from practicing any form of mediation or contemplative activity. Choosing to engage in your favorite activity mindfully and to develop the discipline to continue interacting with it purposefully will allow you to begin to interact with all things throughout your life in that same way.

bare attention

The quality of deliberate focus—also referred to as bare attention—can be thought of as an intense form of paying attention. This is a wonderful metaphor for knitting. As we knit, on some level, we relate exactly to the precision of what our hands are doing. For the new knitter this attention is indeed deliberate, as you slowly and carefully try to make each stitch. You experience the peril of the new loop falling off the tip of the needle, find a comfortable way to let the yarn strand through your fingers and work with the awkward sensations of trying something new. As you become more proficient in your knitting skills these motions become more automatic, drawing attention to the next level. You can start to incorporate a wider perspective, including the drape of the fabric you are making, the interaction of the colors and textures within the yarn, and the essence of what or for whom you are knitting. Even as an advanced knitter, you can use mindful attention to develop a fresh approach toward your work. In meditation this is often referred to as *beginner's mind*. As you return to the viewpoint of bare attention in your knitting experience, try relating to each stitch as a beginner might. This perspective renews our curiosity and reminds us to relate to what is real, not to get carried away in the speed of our skill, the goal of completion, or ideas of how proficient we really are. It lets us notice where our mind is, and brings it back to the needles.

Within the experience of deliberate focus you will find a wonderful opportunity to experience your body and your mind working together, without thoughts and other distractions getting in between them. While your fingers are flying and the yarn is streaming through your hands, perhaps you have hit that place where everything seems balanced and in synch. What is happening in that place? Nothing stands between your intention and the movement of your hands to create fabric. Are you thinking, or are you directly experiencing your world? This amazing synergy of body, mind, yarn, and tools provides one of those special sensations that knitters may be able to recognize, but that mindful knitters are able to define. Next time you feel in synch, pay attention! Feel the yarn sliding through your hands, understand the movement of your needles as directed by your intellect, and use this contemplative space to experience being in the moment and in your body with calm state of mind.

the gifts of irritation and boredom

Inevitably, as we knit, we become aware of our own patience, or sometimes our impatience. In becoming a mindful knitter, you can begin to explore this notion more acutely. When you work on a sweater, sometimes you just can't do it—you don't have the focus, you can't manage to make the project flow. Exploring our discomfort, although unpleasant and sometimes scary, is perhaps one of the more compassionate things we can do for ourselves. So instead of throwing the project down and getting back to it maybe in a day—or maybe in a month—allow yourself the kindness to explore and learn from what's really going on. Maybe you just hate that pattern or that yarn. But maybe as you sit there forming your stitches and noticing what arises, you realize a recurring thought indicating that you find little fulfillment in the project because you're making it for someone you really don't like. Perhaps you don't really hate the sweater; you hate your job.

These things might seem like "gimmies," but how often do we ignore the obvious problems in our lives—even if they're painful—because the familiar feels safe? Once we've made the decision to engage in mindful activity and experience ourselves and our world more acutely, exploring our patience and our habits allows us to stumble upon little bits of self-discovery. Learning this about ourselves is not always easy. Once the proverbial can of worms is open, it becomes our inescapable job to pay attention. But remember, worms produce fertile soil. Acknowledging habits and underlying irritations opens the door for us to view these and all situations as opportunities. If you simply throw the sweater into a bag or switch on the TV and zone out while you continue to work on it, you are delaying inevitable realizations that could benefit your life right now. As we work with disciplines of mindfulness—such as various forms of meditation—we begin to see that every single moment can act as a teacher if we fully engage with it and allow it to teach us. Then, suddenly, as if out of nowhere, we see options and are empowered with choices. This can indeed happen while knitting, if you develop knitting as a tool for cultivating mindfulness.

Also built into the process of knitting is a great gift—the gift of boredom. You may never have thought of being bored as a gift, but boredom is a great teacher, for through it we can learn about our own capacities. Next time you feel bored as you knit, take it as an opportunity presented to you as a contemplative practitioner. Does your boredom show you its clearly defined limits? Perhaps those limits aren't so clear, but rather kind of soft. Is your sense of boredom one of impatience or edginess? Is it simply a matter of wishing you were outside enjoying the sunshine, or is there something more underneath your feeling of squirminess, something that your ever-so-skillful mind is working on overtime to keep you from seeing? You may be on the verge of a breakthrough if you can just stay still and be with it a few minutes more.

One of boredom's great lessons is that it reminds us to stay curious. When we remember to experience boredom with a spirit of adventure, it gives us the gift of learning how to move through a situation by staying with it instead of constantly banging up against it or leaving it until later. Truly experiencing boredom puts us right in the present moment. When we try to escape our boredom, we go off in our thoughts and lose track of the present moment. But, if we welcome boredom as an invitation to curiosity, we can really notice—really look at what is taking place right now. In mediation, this is a gateway to developing mindfulness. In mindful knitting, it is an invitation to practice our focus deliberately and watch what evolves and grows from our needles.

enjoying the process

In contemplative traditions, there is a lot of focus on "right now." But think about this, as cliché as it sounds: what else is there? Many meditation traditions remind us that the past is memory and the future fantasy, so you really should take advantage of your ability to experience what is happening right now, which is where all experience happens. This very philosophical concept also makes very basic sense. This concept of "nowness"—or completely experiencing what is happening in this instant—is a quality that becomes more distinct the more one engages in mindful disciplines.

Being in the moment is related to process. Knitting provides its practitioners with a unique vehicle for engaging in process—to focus on what is happening now, stitch by stitch, without becoming edgy about getting it done. As we create each loop, the experience of that unique moment leaves an imprint on the resulting fabric. Then, if we notice our feelings in the context of mindfulness practice, we can view them as just that—feelings elicited by thoughts generated by our minds. And much like the sun generates light or clouds generate raindrops, thoughts are just there, part of the situation, neither good nor bad. Relating to all endeavors as process and not obsessively focusing on the goal removes the sense of anxiety and burden to which we can all relate far too easily. By noticing thoughts for what they are, the emotions and worries begin to dissipate. Then we are able to really enjoy the experiences along the way. Beginning to relate to this quality in your knitting opens the door for relating to it in all contexts.

mindfulness instructions for knitting as meditation

1. Look at your schedule and find a span of time in your day that you can mark off in your calendar and dedicate to yourself. Perhaps it means waking up half an hour early, or perhaps it means deciding to take your lunch break alone. Schedule this as a very important meeting with yourself.

2. Have an uncomplicated piece of knitting on hand. It could be the project for this chapter, Deliberate Focus Garter Stitch Scarf, or it could be something already on the needles. As you insert the needle into the first stitch, focus on it with your total attention. Very deliberately wrap the yarn around the needle, and pull the new stitch through. Do it again. If it feels like you are exaggerating your movements, that's okay. Do it again.

3. As you start to become comfortable and relax, notice whether your mind wanders off. Very gently state to yourself, "thinking," just as you did in the meditation exercise of the previous chapter when you labeled thoughts with this simple acknowledgment that your mind was doing its thing. Do not feel compelled to assign any particular importance to one thought over another. Simply return your attention to the formation of the stitches, the feel of the needles, and the sensation of the yarn in your hands. Continue knitting and keep gently reminding yourself to return to your knitting and the formation of your stitches. Continue to be kind to yourself.

4. Notice what's happening around you. Notice if your thoughts assume a certain quality or theme during this session. Notice if you are engaging in a period of synchronicity where thought is unnecessary or absent. Just notice whatever is coming up and label it as "thinking," then return to the formation of your stitches and the work on your needles. Notice that

you are quiet and still and see what happens in this very moment as you wrap your yarn, pull through a new stitch, and do it again.

5. One of the great joys of mindful knitting is the tactile and physical qualities of the experience. As a pleasant side benefit, it is a productive endeavor, rewarding you with a physical product as a result of your time spent in mindful activity. As you continue to work, return your attention again and again to the physical sensations of your knitting, using this focus and awareness to bring you back to your actual experience, and back to the present moment. Try to engage in this exercise for at least twenty minutes.

PROJECT: DELIBERATE FOCUS GARTER STITCH SCARF

As you knit this quickie scarf you are invited to cultivate your deliberate focus. Worked in garter stitch—knitting every stitch, knitting every row—this project is a perfect vehicle both for developing solid knitting skills and for creating mindful focus. By supplying a repetitive focusing tool at its most basic level—much like following one's breath in and out—this project invites you to make the transition from mindless knitting to mindful knitting, transforming you into a contemplative knitter.

instructions for mindful knitting

1. As you knit this scarf, as in the previous meditation exercise, give yourself at least twenty minutes of uninterrupted time.
2. If you want to stop after ten minutes, don't. Keep knitting and explore your feelings of boredom. Engage your curiosity and see if it elicits synchronicity between your hands and your mind.
3. The irregular texture of the yarn and the unpredictable color pattern created by the multiple colors invite you to find a synergy as you knit and apply your curiosity as if a puzzle were unfolding in front of your eyes.
4. Use your burgeoning understanding of mindfulness to stay in the present moment as each stitch is formed.

reading a knitting pattern

Reading a knitting pattern is a lot like following a recipe. All the ingredients you will need are clearly stated at the beginning, and the order in which to add them to the mix is spelled out. The pattern here for the Deliberate Focus Garter Stitch Scarf is a great introduction to understanding a pattern.

First you will see a statement of the finished size. If the pattern is for a garment with more than one size, pick the size that is the right fit for your recipient. When more than one size is offered, the alternate information is shown in parentheses—for example, "small (medium, large)." This means that throughout the pattern, the numbers that relate to the size you have chosen will be given in this order. So if you are making a small, you only pay attention to the first set of numbers in front of the parentheses; if you are making a large, you only read the last set of numbers inside the parentheses.

The next entries are the yarn, the needles, the notions, and the gauge for the project. The materials listing is a straightforward itemization of ingredients. (If you need help finding these items or wish for someone to explain to you what a stitch holder is, for example, please consult your local yarn shop.) Next comes a list of techniques used, with page references directing you to fuller explanations of these techniques in case you need further details about them.

The gauge is a very important component of your project. The gauge information in the pattern tells you how many stitches and rows you need to achieve in your knitted swatch to make the project come out the intended size. Gauge is typically given in a measurement of 4 square inches, (10 square centimeters in metric). To ensure accuracy when working your gauge swatch, cast on more stitches than the number you actually need to measure. More about this can also be found in the Tips and Techniques section on page 110.

Following the general instructions, the final entries in the pattern may offer variations or optional additions for the project. Just as for a recipe for baking or cooking, it's a good idea to read through the entire pattern before you begin so you can look up anything that is unclear. But don't try too hard to understand everything thoroughly before you begin; some things simply will not be obvious until you have the stitches on the needles.

Note that measurements and needles sizes are given in Imperial/American measurements, followed by metric inside the parentheses. As with the pattern size, here too you should follow the number set that relates to you.

Often a lot of the information in a knitting pattern may appear to be written in some kind of secret code. Many of the common knitting abbreviations and shorthand have been eliminated from the patterns in this book, and the full words or phrases are used to make things easier to understand. Nonetheless, if an abbreviation is unclear, look it up in the glossary (see page 105). If you need further explanation of a technique or term, please consult a good knitting reference book, or ask your knitting mentor for assistance.

Many projects in this book are also accompanied by two wonderful visual tools for understanding the construction and techniques of a project more intuitively: a schematic, and charts or diagrams when relevant. The schematic—the little diagram showing you the overall shape and dimension of the garment or project when is it complete and assembled—can be invaluable in helping you determine what size to make. Charts are given when the instructions include a basic texture or color stitch pattern. For more detailed instructions on reading charts, please consult the Tips and Techniques section on page 112–113. Diagrams are given as visual reference and suggestions for embroidered or added touches when an embellishment or a motif is part of the project.

GARTER STITCH SCARF

FINISHED SIZE: Ranges 6–10" (15–25.5 cm) wide and 45–72" (114.5–183 cm) long. Scarf shown measures 8" (20.5 cm) wide and 60" (152.5 cm) long.

YARN: 2–3 skeins multicolored or hand-painted textured chunky-weight wool or wool blend. Ask your local yarn shop owner for bulky yarns in this range. Shown in Artful Yarns Circus, color #7 Palm Reader (95% wool, 5% acrylic; 93 yards [85 meters]/100 grams): 2 skeins for scarf pictured.

NEEDLES: US 11 to 15 (8 mm to 10 mm), or size to give gauge as recommended on the wrapper of your chosen yarn.

NOTIONS: Scissors, yarn needle.

GAUGE: 8 to 14 sts = 4" (10 cm) in Garter Stitch. Check your gauge before you begin. Look at the wrapper of your chosen yarn, or ask your local yarn shop owner. It is always best to knit a test swatch before beginning a project—to learn the qualities of the yarn, see how the colors look and to discover or verify the knitted gauge.

See page 57 ▶

TECHNIQUES USED: Casting On (page 106), Garter Stitch (page 109), Binding Off (page 106).

Instructions

Loosely cast on 20 stitches. Work in garter stitch until scarf is desired length or you have used all your yarn. Bind off all stitches. Note: To ensure that you have enough yarn to bind off, begin the bind-off row when the length of yarn remaining is at least five times the width of the stitches on the needle. Weave in the ends.

VARIATIONS: For a longer scarf, add another skein. For a narrower scarf, cast on only 12 stitches.

chapter three

THE WORLD IS FULL of very simple and magical experiences. Participating in them can be much like catching a glimpse of a shooting star—you must be open to them happening. You can't focus on one spot too long; you have to open your peripheral vision to the possibilities. Throughout our day and our lives, we often gloss over the moments of magic and dismiss as mundane and ordinary the things that might in fact be the most rich. As practitioners of a mindful activity, however, we are developing our skill to discern and to refine our appreciation for simplicity and stillness. We understand the restorative power of working a few rows at the end of a long, tiring day. We know that in those few moments of calm, we find a moment to make friends with ourselves. As we extend this point of view to the world, we can reexamine what we consider to be a luxury and what we view as an indulgence. We also find that we can use our mindful focus and our craft to transform the ordinary into the extraordinary.

magic in the moment

Take a closer look at what makes up your world, your life, and your daily routine. On the surface, our lives are defined by what we do, and how we think of ourselves, our schedule, and our habits. Wake up at 6:45, get dressed, off to work, off to school. This structure of our experience continues throughout the day—check our e-mail, lunch at 1:00, dinner at 6:00, a favorite TV program at 8:00, off to bed, and all over again. But what's under the surface? Is it raining today? Did your kid give you a big kiss when she got out of bed? How wonderful did the hot shower feel this morning? What did the food you ate for lunch really taste like? We get so wrapped up in our habits—both habits of schedule and habits of our mind—that our mind is comfortable with the predictability of schedule. It is comfortable with familiar objects—comfortable enough to take them for granted.

On the other hand, if we no longer take the comforts our daily life for granted, we can see that what we perceive as the most mundane thing can in fact be the source of our most profound enjoyment. When we take a moment to slow down our daily schedule and focus on what is happening right now, it stops our minds. In place of obsessing about a confrontation at the office or an upcoming deadline, we can see that at that very moment the sun is shining, or that the coffee is particularly tasty, and this makes us smile.

Consider that cup of coffee, for instance. When we first wake up, nothing much is happening as we orient ourselves to beginning the day. Our bodies move slowly and our thoughts are sleepy. We reach for that cup of coffee, eagerly awaiting the warmth and the richness of its taste. As you lift the cup to your mouth, chances are you are totally focused on the full sensation of the experience. Not a lot of thought is going on—your intention and your actions are working in tandem. Without realizing it, you are experiencing the synchronicity of body and mind. Your mind is not really switched on yet. It is, in fact, right there in that moment and that coffee tastes and feels so good! In the space of fully experiencing that exact moment, you have touched the magic available in every moment.

Do you look forward to this moment every day? Do you prefer to experience it alone? Does this experience resonate within other situations throughout your day? Some people may connect with this magical aspect of body and mind in harmony through a morning run; for others it may be watching the sunrise, or perhaps knitting a few rows. Regardless of what takes you to that point, you experience a profound sense of simply being and relaxing right there. Just being fully present in that moment encourages us to relax, to lighten up, and enjoy the fact that we are here. In that moment of synchronicity we are invited to shift our perspective on what's really consequential, and what is, in fact, irrelevant.

What about cultivating this experience throughout your day? Not only can we find this experience in what we might consider the most mundane activities, but it is through these ordinary tasks that the experience may be most rich. We know that we can find this experience through knitting, but can we also find it while gardening, doing dishes, fixing dinner, or watching our kids play at the playground? Really, we can find it absolutely everywhere, whenever our minds and bodies are opening together completely in the present moment.

Interestingly, this place of "present moment" is one that our minds seem to find innately uncomfortable. Our minds constantly and instinctively move away, escaping into webs of story lines, shopping lists, and daydreams, seeking comfort in the distraction. Yet, as we know first-hand from that first sip of morning coffee, soothing comfort can also be found right there, right now, fully, as we choose to relish our direct interaction with what is going on. Engaging more and more with direct experience sheds new light on the ordinary. We can begin see the world as a secure, supportive place. When stripped down to the moment-by-moment experience of being, our lives offer us profound yet simple joys.

These little magic moments of grace are inherent in all the things we do, but it is easiest to find them at home. As we examine our daily routine, we can find opportunities to interject reminders for ourselves to stay in that moment and feel the connection between mind and body. Such a reminder may be an object of significance we place at the kitchen windowsill, or a dish towel given to us as a gift. As we participate in our habitual activities, we can remind ourselves to notice the presence of these tools, and they in turn remind us to bring our attention to our experience, letting thoughts fall away.

Similarly, we can cultivate this sense of grace in the way we conduct our daily activities. By simplifying our processes—stripping them down—we grant ourselves the opportunity to fully appreciate what we have and the experience of having it. This could be the ritual of a hot bath after a long day, or making a point to have fresh flowers on the dining table, with the commitment to look at them and enjoy their beauty. It could also be getting out your grandmother's silver sugar bowl and using it. Commit yourself to keeping it shiny and beautiful, polishing it when necessary and enjoying its elegance and the connection it brings you to a time or person you love. We choose to cultivate these reminder tools and develop our willingness to use them to prompt ourselves to stay right here and feel the warmth of the sun, listen to the sounds of the wind or the traffic, and feel our breathing as a constant companion.

touching the basic goodness of being

The essence of that sense of grace—that little bit of "ordinary magic" inherent within the experience of each moment—can be referred to as basic goodness, which is inherent in all things. Although basic goodness is a principle fundamental to the Shambhala perspective as presented in depth by Chögyam Trungpa Rinpoche, it is by no means unique to the Buddhist point of view. It is a natural state of being. It is not good in the sense of good compared to bad; it is good in the sense that is it is always available and present in every person, every experience, and every moment whether we are able to connect with it or not. Basic goodness is the place within us where we realize the promise and potential of our life, whatever state it's in. Basic goodness embodies the capacity within all things and all situations to wake us up and invites us to contribute to the situation —be it a dinner conversation, a joyful moment, or an act of kindness. And the really powerful twist to basic goodness is that if we acknowledge it and work with it within ourselves, it extends outward from us to the world. When we begin to see that every person, living creature, or situation we encounter holds within the same potential, the experience becomes very powerful.

How can we experience basic goodness in seemingly common experiences, such as washing the dishes or knitting? We can take pride in having a clean place to eat. We can appreciate the warm water and the scents of the kitchen. We can fully feel the tactile sensations of the yarn as it moves through our hands. We can fill ourselves with the essence of the person for whom we are knitting. We can listen acutely to the sounds out the window as we knit or cook.

When we see the basic goodness in these simple activities, we are reminded to return to the moment. In this space of right now, we can appreciate our environment, we can appreciate what we have, we can appreciate just being here. By nourishing ourselves in this way, we encourage ourselves to stay present—right here with the warm water, the cooking smells, the feel and color of the yarn. It is up to you to wake up to this ordinary magic inherent in all things.

simpleness

Cultivating our ability to see things as flashes of ordinary magic allows us to truly deepen our appreciation for what we experience and what we have. By simplifying our definitions of what is important and what is magical, our relationship with our world and ourselves begins to grow stronger and more profound, reavealing a lush richness and sense of wonder. Our ideas about what is necessary and what is a blessing grow and change. We may find that they are one and the same.

Through the lens of simplicity we can experience the magic in things that we might have otherwise taken for granted. We begin to see this kind of magic unfold everywhere—in hugging a child, getting into a freshly made bed, or sitting down to knit at the end of a long day. We may find it when we come across a parking spot with money already in the meter, or as we savor the taste of fine, rich chocolate.

Cultivating these qualities and experiences—bringing them beyond a chance experience, or a fleeting occasional acknowledgment—brings them into a purposeful realm that we can use to enhance our lives. Through our developing relationship with mindfulness, we can intentionally develop awareness of really being present with our experience. In this way we increasingly notice that we are touching that magic inside every moment. As we go to that magic spot more and more, we begin to touch essence of basic goodness. We can do this by engaging in formal sitting meditation practice, or by fully engaging in everyday activities in a simplified fashion—a walk, housework, or knitting with deliberate focus.

This deepening appreciation invites us to further explore simplicity—simplicity in our state of mind, in our thoughts and actions, and in the things we have and how we use them. From the viewpoint of a mindfulness practitioner, we begin to see that our choices to stay simple can be really enriching. We can make the choice not to contribute confusion and added chaos to situations that arise. We can be aware of skillfully choosing our words when communicating with another person. We can choose not to focus on unnecessary worries and unnecessary things. As we peel away the complexities, a glimpse of calm and sanity reveals itself. In this sanity we can find that simple state of basic goodness and ordinary magic.

Working with the ideas of magic and simplicity helps us explore and redefine our ideas about indulgence. As we actively engage with a sense of goodness and magic in the world, our view of indulgence can be redefined as something very positive. We can invite ourselves to indulge in our lives. We can indulge in our authentic experience. We can indulge in magic, delighting in synchronicity. We indulge in what we already have, and what we do every day. From this point of view, indulgence is not extravagant or excessive, but an opportunity for us to be thankful and to extend kindness and gentleness toward ourselves. We can invite the mundane to transform into the delightful. Such a simple perspective allows us to stop looking around outside for contentment and to more fully appreciate what we have, and what we have to offer.

We can use our relationship with how we knit, and how we knit mindfully, to invite such a shift in our perspective. We can use what we knit and our minds and our sensations as we knit to explore our concept of the duality of abundance and simplicity. As knitters we have the skill to transform our intention and our time into tangible things—creating fabric from yarn. As mindful knitters, we have the opportunity to expand our love of our craft to exploring the essence of magic as we challenge the roles of the things we make and the things we hold dear. We can develop a deepening appreciation for our time and the good fortune of our circumstances. We can explore our ideas about what's important and what really delights us as we, through our intention, transform something that may have once been considered mundane into something treasured. We may discover renewed joy in slipping on a pair of hand-knit socks on a cold morning, or using a super-soft, lovingly hand-knit cloth to enhance our otherwise basic, daily routines. Better yet, we can invite others to discover this newfound joy for themselves.

Project: A Trio of Washcloths

Our newly deconstructed concept of luxury allows us to view our daily routine as holding little pleasures. A magically ordinary knitting project—a washcloth—is a functional item, a necessary object. Yet through the process of making one with our own hands, its function and its role in our lives can be examined. Take the initiative of creating and using this reminder tool to stay present by deliberately crafting one with your own hands.

The project presented in this chapter is a trio of hand-knit washcloths—soft, thick chenille cloths that can be used for daily routine. The exercise of creating and using these simple yet indulgent cloths invites you to connect with the basic goodness in yourself and your experience, then allows it to radiate outward through your interactions with others, or your choice to make these cloths as a gift.

The first of the trio of cloths is knit in garter stitch. This is a good place to start and build on the mindful knitting meditation instruction from the previous chapter. Begin by placing your focus on the rhythmic formation of the stitch. Notice how the chenille feels in your hands—it's soft and velvety, a little fragile. Continue to focus on these tactile sensations and the deliberate movements of your hands as they wrap each stitch. As you proceed to create fabric from individual stitches, experience what it feels like to touch the magic in the experience of the moment. Perhaps you do this by connecting with your current surroundings, or perhaps by connecting with the love you feel for the person for whom you are knitting. Try to stay within this sensation; if your attention wanders, gently bring yourself back to your deliberate focus on the formation of the stitches and the fabric. Use the sensations in your body to remind you of your place in the moment, and notice if you experience the rich sensation of the synchronization of your body and your intention.

Knit from textured stitches, the other two cloths require slightly more concentration on the technical aspects of the patterns. Should you seek knitting that is a little more of challenge than the introductory garter stitch scarf project, you may choose to begin with the second cloth offered. It may be helpful to introduce one element at a time. After you cast on, you may wish to work through the first one or two repeats of the stitch pattern in your cloth before you begin to work with the mindfulness mediation aspect. Once you are familiar with the rhythm of the stitch sequence, proceed as explained above, bringing your attention to the physical sensations and noticing when your mind wanders away from what is happening in your hands. I find it very helpful to take a loose, intuitive approach to knitting basic stitch patterns such as the checkerboard and the rice stitch. For the checkerboard pattern, instead of getting wrapped up in how many rows you have completed or what numbered stitch you are on, notice how the fabric looks. The knitting will visually tell you what to do next. Does the square you are working on look to be about the same height as the previous one? If so, then it's probably time to change to the next sequence. For the rice stitch, notice the built-in metronome of right-side and wrong-side rows that can keep your pattern on track. (See "Tip for Intuitive Knitting" on page 33.)

Follow the mindful knitting instructions while knitting these lovely everyday treasures.

Perhaps you are knitting a cloth for a baby, working in soft chenille to caress the little one's sweet, sensitive skin. Perhaps you are knitting a cloth for a friend who does not allow herself indulgences and would benefit tremendously from the alchemy that takes place between a hand-knit washcloth, handmade aromatic soap, and a hot bath. Or perhaps this is for you, to wash the supper dishes or as a facecloth at the end of the day—a reminder tool to keep it simple and keep it kind. Made from a pure, natural, soft yarn, this simple object is elevated to a luxury, allowing both its creator and its user to redefine the most mundane things as indulgences.

instructions for mindful knitting

1. Take a comfortable seat where you can sit upright with your feet squarely on the floor. Feel the sense of taking your place. Let your focus rest on the rhythmic formation of the stitch. Enjoy the tactile sensation of the soft fiber stranding through your hands.

2. Dwell in the experience of simplicity and work with the notion of touching the magic in the moment by connecting with your surroundings and your physical sensation. Explore your connection to basic goodness and the sentiment you have for the person for whom you are knitting.

3. After working a few rows, notice if your mind wanders. Are you staying in your current circumstance, or have you gone off to another place entirely? Gently come back to your work and the sensation of the yarn in your hands.

4. Remember to introduce one element at a time working through the one or two repeats of the stitch pattern, then returning to the mindfulness mediation instruction when you are ready.

5. Explore the notion of synchronicity of mind and body. Continue to softly remind yourself to connect to the moment and nourish yourself, your growing confidence, and your experience of upliftedness. Dwell in the richness of the ordinary in all things. Gently return your attention to the formation of the stitches to remind you of your place in the moment. Continue to use your deliberate focus on the act of knitting as your tool for mindful focus.

tip for intuitive knitting:
right side/wrong side and the telltale tail

The sequence of many simple knit-and-purl stitch patterns depends on attention to the right side (front) and wrong side (back) of the knitted fabric to make the pattern unfold properly. In the first few rows of the pattern instructions, the abbreviations RS (right side) and WS (wrong side) indicate which side will face out. This is always very important, but especially so when a stitch pattern is identical on both the front and back. Tracking rows with a row counter can be very laborious and detracts from the inherent intuitive quality of knitting. For an easy and intuitive way to quickly determine whether the row you are about to knit is a right- or wrong-side row, try this trick, which assumes that row one and all odd rows of your pattern are right-side rows.

Cast on using the Two-Tail or Long Tail Cast-On method (sometimes also called the Double Cast-On; see page 107). Note that this trick will not work with other methods of casting on. If you are not sure what row you are on, place your knitting down on the table when you are about to begin a row. Point the tip of the left-hand needle toward your right-hand side, just as it will be when you pick it up to knit. Glance down to the cast-on of your work. If the cast-on tail is on the right-hand side of the piece, you are about to begin a right-side row. If the tail is on the left-hand side, you are beginning a wrong-side row.

▲ *See page 58*

tip for intuitive knitting: rest rows

One of my favorite aspects of textured knitting, the rest row allows the knitter simply to work back across the row, knitting the knits and purling the purls as they appear. This feature, usually worked on a wrong-side row of a combination or cable stitch, allows a break from concentration and opportunity to tune rhythmically into to the meditation technique. Rest rows (and wrong-side rows in general) also provide a natural knitting metronome, helping the intuitive knitter track how many sets of a pattern have been completed, or foretelling an action to take place on the next row.

A Trio of Washcloths

Create a simple pleasure, both in the knitting and in the use of these delightful handmade cloths. Very easy to knit, these projects provide a transformative tool both for mindful knitting as well as for growing knitting skills. Progressing from the first through the third version requires slightly increased levels of concentration.

The first cloth, though very basic, is made luxurious with soft, velvety cotton chenille. A continuation of the deliberate focus exercise in the previous project, it is the most straightforward to knit and allows the knitter to continue practicing raw focus on the knit stitch as meditation tool.

The simple knit and purl stitch combination of the second cloth creates a thick, scrubby fabric similar to a waffle weave. To knit the rice stitch, you will employ the technique of knitting in the back of the loop. This stitch pattern has an obvious front and back, and can be worked in a very intuitive manner by enjoying the notion of rest rows. (See "Tip for Intuitive Knitting" on this page.) Requiring a little more concentration than basic garter stitch, this stitch allows the mindful knitter to integrate a simple level of concentration into their practice.

The stitch used for the third cloth creates a rich, decorative texture with checkered blocks of knit and purl. Calling for the most concentration of the three washcloth patterns, this stitch requires the knitter to track stitches across the row as well as to alternate the pattern blocks every five rows. A project such as this small, quick-to-knit square provides the mindful knitter a safe place to integrate a meditative focus with cognitive tracking of knitting technique.

FINISHED SIZE: Approximately 10–11" (25.5–28 cm) square.

YARN: Crystal Palace Cotton Chenille, color #1015 Natural (100% cotton; 98 yards [90 meters]/50 grams): 3 skeins for 3 washcloths. The garter and checkerboard cloths take slightly more than 1 skein, the rice stitch cloth slightly less.

NEEDLES: US 6 (4 mm), or size to give gauge.

NOTIONS: Scissors, yarn needle.

GAUGE: Approximately 19 sts = 4" (10 cm) in different patterns, or whatever produces a densely knit fabric of your liking. Check your gauge before you begin.

TECHNIQUES USED: Casting On (page 106), Reading Pattern Charts (page 112), Binding Off (page 106).

Washcloth One Instructions: Garter Stitch

Cast on 50 stitches. Knit every row until the cloth is roughly ½" (1.3 cm) longer than it is wide. Loosely bind off all stitches. Weave in the ends. Machine wash and dry for tight, fluffy fabric.

Washcloth Two Instructions: Rice Stitch

Cast on 51 stitches. Work Rice Stitch pattern as follows:
Row 1: (RS) P1, *knit 1 in the back of the loop, rep from * to end.
Row 2: Knit across the row.
Repeat these two rows for pattern until the cloth is roughly ½" (1.3 cm) longer than it is wide, ending on a RS row (meaning that last row you complete is a right-side row). Bind off all stitches loosely on the next WS row. Weave in the ends. Machine wash and dry for tight, fluffy fabric.

Washcloth Three Instructions: Checkerboard Cloth

Cast on 52 stitches. Work the checkerboard pattern as shown in the chart. Work even in pattern until cloth is roughly ½" (1.3 cm) longer than it is wide, ending with Row 5 or Row 10 of the chart. On the next row, loosely bind off all stitches. Machine wash and dry for tight, fluffy fabric.

▲ *Checkerboard Cloth Chart*

□ knit on right side; purl on wrong side

• purl on right side; knit on wrong side

□ pattern repeat

chapter four

CONNECTING TO THE WORLD:

DISCOVERING THE HEART OF GENEROSITY

THROUGH OUR MINDFUL ACTIVITIES, we first begin to feel our own tender hearts and discover, perhaps to our amazement, that they have a rich capacity to hold joy and sadness. Now that we're finding this quality within our own hearts, we can almost magically begin to see this capacity in others. The bridge for making this connection to others is our deepening understanding of the basic goodness inherent in every moment. As our experience of basic goodness matures, it hits a sort of saturation point, and its focus begins to shift automatically from our inward situation to the world at large.

As we start to pay attention to how we relate to the world mindfully, we instinctively wish to engage with this energy. What, then, can we do? We can respond with generosity. As mindful knitters we can place this generosity in our own knitting practice by creating for others, whether for friends or strangers, as gifts of charity. By exploring the generosity in our knitting we can further deepen our experience in the world. We can also explore this connection in other ways. Perhaps we choose to help by engaging in our community in a way that will alleviate some suffering. Even if our actions feel small, they are valuable. By choosing to engage with others purposefully and mindfully, we can learn from what we see and we can contribute to the well-being of the world, whether our definition of the world is large or small. Just as our notion of basic goodness expands and spills over, so do our mindful actions in the world at large, making it a better place, situation by situation, person by person, stitch by stitch.

the warrior's gentle heart

Once we touch on our own basic goodness and then connect with the basic goodness and magic inherent in every experience, our tender heart begins to pulse. In the Shambhala philosophy, the "heart of generosity" is considered the warrior's heart. In traditional Western thinking, we might consider the heart of a warrior to be cool and steely, perhaps calculating and single-minded. But here, the heart of the warrior is soft, warm, and often a bit squishy. This is the heart that opens and expands. It is the place in us that connects with both the joy and the suffering of the world in an unconditional way. The gentle heart of the warrior is at once radiant and supportive while also weepy and melting. Both of these elements combine to allow us to deeply feel the true essence of compassion—the tears that come from beauty, the connection to everyone and everything—whether it comes through understanding of suffering or of joy.

Our natural tendency may be to close up this kind of heart; it is intense and not always pleasurable. Our minds may instinctively wish to dwell on things that bring us a mainline feeling of joy rather than the bittersweet quality that is more truly the essence of life. But as we have explored, the essence of the open heart and the awake quality of mindfulness are found in directly experiencing whatever arises. The challenge is in working directly with that which our minds may deem undesirable or painful. The warrior finds bravery in his or her direct relationship with what is happening.

Within these experiences, we can try to summon up our bravery and really feel what is happening, not in an indulgent way but in a way that allows us to connect with the very real human condition of simultaneous joy and sadness. This approach contains a quality of seeing things for what they are, and the wisdom of the warrior's heart is to move through these situations without attaching his or her own story lines to the mix, but rather to really feel those feelings, stay present in the moment, and find the basic goodness that dwells in there somewhere.

Basic goodness may be found inside the compassion you yourself are cultivating that allows you to be thankful for your own situation and calls you to action to help another person who is suffering. It may be found in the dignity so radiantly displayed by the person whose life seems, from your perspective, to be as bad as it can possibly be. It may be found in that trembling emotional place that makes our heart both joyful and achy.

As you become more aware of your own basic goodness through engaging in your mindful activity, you may find that you cannot stop your open heart from spilling out. Your connection with this primal element in all situations and all beings has a reverberating, exponential quality. You may begin thinking about people and situations in a new, almost softer way. That softness comes from connecting with basic goodness. You may find yourself instinctively helping someone, which you might never have considered doing before. Simply by being aware of other people and the quality of your interaction with them, your basic goodness becomes both contagious and more powerful. Simply by being aware of other people and the quality of your interaction with them, you contribute to the situation rather than detract from it.

sangha

In its traditional, literal sense, *sangha* means a community of Buddhist practitioners or fellow travelers on the spiritual path. Yet since its use has become more colloquial in contemporary spiritual lingo, it refers to a community of like-minded people with common interests and a common vision. For me this word has come to mean "family" as much as anything else— extended family, meaning the people you pick, not necessarily those to whom you happen to be related by blood. One of the key components of this idea of sangha is that your participation in this particular community and with these particular people is deliberate and purposeful. And just like blood relatives, there are some whom you occasionally might prefer not to have to sit next to, but when you look at them from the standpoint of mindful interaction, perhaps you can become curious about what you might learn. So you invite them in and indulge that curiosity, and your life may become richer.

You may experience many levels of sangha in your world: your neighborhood, your knitting group, your church community, your girlfriends. These various components of your life may overlap, or you may keep them very separate. The common thread in all of these microcosms is that you are a participant and that you have something to bring to the party. Hopefully what you bring is something that makes the party a little more enjoyable. Your contribution to each of these realms may fluctuate—sometimes you are there to entertain, sometimes to teach, and sometimes to learn, and sometimes just to listen. Your contribution may even be gently reminding others to stay present and make his or her own contributions. If you are participating mindfully, each interaction will be genuine and the situation as a whole will be worthwhile for everyone.

Within each of these and in all situations, the magic of sangha—of a group of people purposefully and deliberately interacting with one another—is the power it has to act as a container for the mutual experience. The word *container* is often used in the context of intensive spiritual study and practice, and it literally means something that supports you when you need it. It also implies that when you are not the one in need, you extend the favor to others. Each of your sanghas, whether spiritually oriented or not, probably abides by this sort of unspoken rule. It's something that "girlfriends" instinctively know all about—the give and receive.

enlightened society

The Shambhala philosophies of basic goodness and enlightened society are inspired by the ancient legend of the Kingdom of the Shambhala. Perhaps real, perhaps mythical, Shambhala is said to have existed high in the Tibetan plateau centuries ago—the basis of the legend of Shangri-La. The society of Shambhala is believed to have been a culture of fearlessness, dignity, and compassion. Its sense of social responsibility and its compassion are believed to be rooted in the practice of meditation. In this view of enlightened society, a fundamental acknowledgment of human dignity, vividness of experience, and recognition of the goodness inherent in all beings represent an ideal for secular society. The Shambhala point of view respects that there is a natural source of radiance and brilliance in the world, the source of which is the innate wakefulness and dignity of all beings. From the Shambhala perspective, each one of us is a fearless warrior, given the opportunity to apply our skills of mindfulness to all we do. In this way, we have the opportunity to inspire others to lead lives of compassion and dignity, and through our own actions and attitudes, improve the condition of the world for all human beings. This view of enlightened society respects and encompasses the wisdom of all cultures and all aspects of civilization, encouraging us to infuse everything with a sense of sacredness.

Enlightened society is an idea of a world built upon generosity and kindness where everyone mindfully contributes to the support and well-being of everyone else. Fundamental to this notion, which is based on the structure said to have existed in the mythical kingdom of Shambhala, is the recognition of the potential within all human beings to wake up to their own basic goodness and contribute to the world. When we make the connection between our own basic goodness within and the magic of the basic goodness without, it touches us and makes our hearts soft and tender. As you awaken to your own basic goodness, you begin to see it everywhere—in everyone, everything, and every moment of the world. It is then that we become warriors. And as you may have already seen in yourself, once you have made that awakening within yourself, you can't help but let it spill out into the world.

What does this have to do with your life? Well, you and I are human beings, so that's the basic point. We are alive and we live in a world full of hurt. Yet despite this, it is in our nature to seek the elements of basic goodness around us, and even in the worst of times they are still there. What if every single person on this planet made the choice to connect with those elements, that sense of magic and space in the moment that we have been developing through our mindfulness practice? It could truly and profoundly change things. Think about what could happen if every person who felt the frustration or pain that is part of being alive was able to do a double take and look at his or her own situation with compassion. Whether you are a janitor or the leader of the free world, your perspective would be invited to shift. In this way, baby step by baby step, the world might really evolve into its full potential.

The very profound component of the concept of enlightened society is how powerful the smallest act can truly be. That single choice you make to have a basically good point of view on your life, or your day, or the fact that your car just broke down, contributes to the entire situation. As we touch others and wake up their sense of basic goodness and compassion through our own actions, the world at large begins to benefit. The smallest action can send out a breath of fresh air to everyone we encounter. The world lightens up a little. As each person feels that little bit of relief—that little encounter with basic goodness and compassion—the world begins to lighten up a lot. Your deliberate and mindful participation makes a difference. Thus, by making the choice to contribute to your world or to offer relief to one other person, you yourself move the world closer to the ideal of enlightened society.

PROJECT: WARM BLANKET AND HATS FOR GIVING

Composed of three items specifically designed to be knitted and given to others, this project enables you to put your knitting needles and your mindful knitting practice into action to make your world and the life of someone else a better place. The set of three knitted pieces—a basic hat for a child, a basic hat for an adult, and a blanket for donation or gift giving—invites you to dwell in the warmth of the heart of generosity and to examine the place of tenderness and compassion within yourself. As knitters know, so much of ourselves is knit into the structure of the fabric, and here that sense of warmth can literally be shared with a loved one or with an appreciative stranger. In this way, you can explore your own capacity for kindness, allowing you to share this kindness more freely.

A super easy project, this trio of a patchwork style blanket, adult rolled-edge hat, and kooky kid's hat can be knocked out quickly, making for great gifts or donations to a shelter, charity, or fund-raising event. All projects are shown here in machine-washable wool. The blanket is worked in five strips, then sewn together when all the strips are done. This makes the project manageable and portable, and allows the knitter to focus on one square at a time without the hassle of sewing individual squares together later. Colors are changed every 6" (15 cm) to form the color blocks.

The adult's rolled-edged hat is knit in the round on circular and double-pointed needles (see page 107). Don't let double-pointed needles scare you. Meeting them like this, in the middle of an established project, is the best way to learn how to use them. Worked in stockinette stitch created by knitting every round, this project provides a great container for contemplative focus, allowing the mindful knitter to infuse the work with the essence of generosity.

The child's colorful rolled-edge hat is also knit in the round on circular and double-pointed needles and joined across the top with a three-needle bind-off (page 115). Shown here with contrasting rolled edge, it can also be knit in a single color or texture pattern. If you're customizing the size of your hats, remember that a hat should be at least 1" (2.5 cm) smaller than the circumference of the wearer's head for a snuggly fit. Suggestions for customizing the fit are also given with the patterns.

instructions for mindful knitting

1. Consider doing a session of sitting meditation for ten or fifteen minutes to quiet your mind and bring your focus into the present. Let go of the tasks and encounters of the day and just be, enlisting the tools of focusing on the breath and labeling thoughts.

2. Begin working following the knitting instructions for this project. Consider whom you will be knitting this for—as a donation, for an elderly friend, for your sister, for a new baby? As you cast on the stitches and start in on the knitting, dwell for a moment in the sensations of what it means to you to give.

3. Enlist your mindful knitting technique, bringing your attention to the formation of the stitches and the physical sensation of the yarn moving through your hands. If the techniques of this project, such as knitting in the round or using double-pointed needles, are new to you, give yourself some time to learn how to use the new tools. Be kind to yourself, and take an adventuresome stance on the project. Once you are comfortable with the tools and techniques, return to your mindful focus.

4. Allow yourself to feel your tender heart. If it makes you cry, then cry. If it makes you giggle, then by all means giggle. Explore the joy in making a gift, and consider the contribution you are making to the situation of the person for whom you are knitting. Hold this contemplation in place for a while, and if you notice your mind drifting off to other things, bring yourself back to the formation of the stitch and the physical sensations of your work.

5. Consider forming a charity knitting group—expand your sangha! Make your compassion and relationship with basic goodness contagious. Invite your knitting friends to discuss their feelings and ideas about giving and generosity during your knitting group meeting times. What kinds of thoughts come up, and what are the commonalities?

BLANKET FOR GIVING

A note about altering the size: If you plan to make the blanket larger, work the desired number of additional blocks to lengthen each strip, then add the same number of additional strips. For example, if you choose to make a 42" (106.5 cm) square blanket, you would work two more 6" (15 cm) blocks in each strip, for a total of seven blocks. To keep the blanket square, you will need to add two strips to the width as well, making the finished blanket a seven x seven grid of color blocks. For a larger blanket you will need more yarn. Plan on each 50-gram ball making approximately two and a half color blocks.

FINISHED SIZE : Blanket shown measures 30" (76 cm) square.

YARN: Mission Falls 1824 Wool (100% Merino superwash wool; 85 yards [78 meters]/50 grams): 4 balls #019 Mist (C1); 5 balls #023 Amethyst (C2); 2 balls #003 Oyster (C3).

NEEDLES: US 8 (5 mm), or size to give gauge.

NOTIONS: Measuring tape, yarn needle, scissors, crochet hook size J (6 mm; optional).

GAUGE: 18 sts and 24 rows = 4" (10 cm) in St St. Check your gauge before you begin.

TECHNIQUES USED: Casting On (page 106), Binding Off (page 106), Stockinette Stitch (page 114).

See page 59 ▶

Please refer to the blanket illustration for color placement.

Instructions

Strip 1 (make 3): With C1, loosely cast on 28 sts. Work in stockinette stitch (St St; knit all sts on RS, purl all sts on WS) for 6" (15 cm), and end having just completed a WS row.

Continuing in St St and changing colors every 6" (15 cm), work four more color blocks in the following order: C2, C1, C2, C1. Loosely bind off all sts. Make two more strips the same as the first. Each strip should measure approximately 6¼" (16 cm) wide and 30" (76 cm) long.

Strip 2 (make 2): With C2, loosely cast on 28 sts. Work in stockinette stitch (St St) for 6" (15 cm), and end having just completed a WS row. Continuing in St St and changing colors every 6" (15 cm), work four more color blocks in the following order: C3, C2,

▼ *Blanket for Giving Chart*

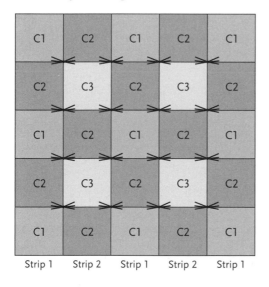

| Strip 1 | Strip 2 | Strip 1 | Strip 2 | Strip 1 |

C3, C2. Loosely bind off all sts. Make another strip the same as the first. Each strip should measure approximately 6¼" (16 cm) wide and 30" (76 cm) long.

Finishing: Weave in the ends. Arrange the strips as shown in the illustration and invisibly sew them together side by side.

EMBELLISHMENTS: The blanket shown features both of the following optional embellishments.

Ties: Cut sixteen 8" (20.5 cm) lengths of each color. Thread a yarn needle with three strands together (one each of all three colors). Take one stitch at the intersection where four blocks meet, and tie the ends evenly in an overhand knot on the RS. Trim the ends to approximately 2" (5 cm) long. Repeat for remaining intersections as shown.

Edging: Using the color of your choice, work blanket stitch embroidery or a row of single crochet around the outer edge. The blanket shown has a single crochet edging of Mist (C1).

customizing the hat
by reading the ball band

Make sure you have about 150–200 yards (137.16–182.88 meters) of yarn on hand. Select a needle size appropriate to your chosen yarn; refer to the ball band or ask your local yarn shop owner for guidance in selecting needle size. Determine the gauge of your yarn, again by referring to the ball band or asking the shop owner. Decide on your desired finished circumference, remembering that the hat should be at least 1" (2.5 cm) smaller than the head circumference of the wearer. Now multiply the number of stitches to the inch in your yarn gauge by the desired circumference. You will want the resulting number to be divisible by 2 in order to work the three-needle bind-off. Here's an example for bulky yarn:

Gauge: 3 sts = 1" (2.5 cm)

Recommended needle size: US 10½ (6.5 mm)

Desired finished size: 19"

(Desired finished size) x (sts per inch) = number of sts to cast on, rounding up to an even number if necessary.

In this example, 19" x 3 stitches per inch means that you should cast 58 stitches (57 rounded up to an even number) onto a US 10½ (6.5 mm) circular needle, and work according to the hat directions given.

the better join

To avoid having a gap in your work when you begin your first round of circular knitting, knit the first stitch very tightly with the yarn coming from the last stitch cast on. Then continuing knitting around and around until your work is the desired length.

ADULT HAT FOR GIVING

FINISHED SIZE: To fit average adult, approximately 21" (53.5 cm) around.

YARN: Mission Falls 1824 Wool (100% Merino superwash wool; 85 yards [78 meters]/50 grams): 2 balls #21 Denim.

NEEDLES : US 8 (5 mm) circular, 16" (40 cm) long, or size to give gauge.
US 8 (5 mm) set of four double-pointed needles, or size to give gauge.

NOTIONS: Measuring tape, yarn needle, scissors, stitch marker (optional).

GAUGE: 18 sts and 24 rows = 4" (10 cm) in St St. Check your gauge before you begin.

TECHNIQUES USED: Casting On (page 106), Joining Work to Knit in the round (page 111), Tail (Cast-On Tail) as Marker (page 115), Stockinette Stitch (page 114), Working with Double-Pointed Needles (page 108), Decreasing (page 108), Ribbing (optional; page 113).

Instructions

With circular needle, loosely cast on 96 sts. Mark the beginning of your round either by placing a stitch marker on the needle when you complete your cast-on, or by using the cast-on tail to indicate where one round ends and the next begins.

▲ *See page 59*

Join the work in a circle, being careful not twist; in other words, make sure that the stitches are not twisting around the needle. If arranged correctly, all the bumps from your cast-on will lie along the same edge of the circular needle, facing in toward the center of the circle. If you choose to do so, mark the beginning of the round and knit the first stitch to close the circle.

Work even in stockinette stitch in the round (St St; knit all sts every rnd) until hat measures approximately 8" (20.5 cm) from the cast-on, or 2" (5 cm) less than desired length. Rearrange the stitches evenly on three double-pointed needles, 32 sts on each needle.

Begin decreasing for top of hat as follows:
Decrease Rnd 1: *Knit 6 sts, k2tog; repeat from * to end of rnd—84 sts.
Knit 1 rnd even.
Decrease Rnd 2: *Knit 5 sts, k2tog; repeat from * to end of rnd—72 sts.
Knit 1 rnd even.
Decrease Rnd 3: *Knit 4 sts, k2tog; repeat from * to end of rnd—60 sts.
Knit 1 rnd even.

Continue in this manner, working the decrease rnd every other rnd, and knitting one stitch less before the k2tog on each decrease rnd, until 24 sts remain. Knit 1 rnd even. On the next rnd, k2tog all the way around—12 sts. Cut yarn, leaving a 12" (30.5 cm) tail. Thread through yarn needle and draw through remaining sts. Fasten securely. Weave in the ends on WS.

VARIATIONS: See "Customizing the Hat by Reading the Ball Band" on page 46.

Larger hat: Use bulky yarn (3 or 4 sts = 1" [2.5 cm]) and larger needles (check the ball band for appropriate size). Follow pattern above, adding 1–2" (2.5–5 cm) to the overall length before beginning the decreases.

Smaller hat: Use DK or light worsted yarn (5 or 6 sts = 1"[2.5 cm]) and smaller needles (again, check the ball band for size). Follow pattern above, eliminating 1–2" (2.5–5 cm) from the overall length before beginning the decreases.

Striped hat: For a classic look, change colors at regular intervals, such as every four rows, or make random stripes for a funky look. If you are changing colors every four rows or less, leave the unused colors attached and carry them up the inside of the hat until they are needed again to eliminate unnecessary ends.

Cuffed brim hat (watch cap style): Work in ribbing (page 113) for 3" (7.5 cm), or about twice the desired depth of the folded brim. Change to St St and follow the pattern above. To measure the height of the hat before decreasing, fold up the brim and measure from the base of the fold.

CHILD'S HAT FOR GIVING

FINISHED SIZE: To fit 18 months to 4 years, approximately 19" (48.5 cm) around.

YARN: Mission Falls 1824 Wool (100% Merino superwash wool; 85 yards [78 meters]/50 grams): two balls main color (MC); one ball contrast color (CC); 3–4 yards (2.74–3.66 meters) of third color for braided tassels (optional). Shown in #023 Amethyst (MC), #019 Mist (CC), and #003 Oyster.

NEEDLES: US 8 (5mm) circular needle, 16" (40 cm) long, or size to give gauge.

NOTIONS: Measuring tape, yarn needle, scissors, spare single or double-pointed needle US 8 (5mm) for three-needle bind-off, stitch marker (optional).

GAUGE: 18 sts and 24 rows = 4" (10 cm) in St St. Check your gauge before you begin.

TECHNIQUES USED: Casting On (page 106), Joining Work to Knit in the Round (page 111), Tail (Cast-on Tail) as a Marker (page 115), Stockinette Stitch (page 114), Three-Needle Bind-Off (page 115). See "The Better Join" on page 47.

Instructions

With CC and circular needle, loosely cast on 86 sts. You will need to mark the beginning of your round either by placing a stitch marker on the needle when you complete your cast-on, or by using the cast-on tail to indicate where one round ends and the next begins.

Join the work in a circle, being careful not twist; in other words, make sure that the stitches are not twisting around the needle. If arranged correctly, all the bumps from your cast-on will lie along the same edge of the circular needle, facing in toward the center of the circle. If you choose to do so, mark the beginning of the round and knit the first stitch to close the circle.

Work even in stockinette stitch in the round (St St; knit all sts every round) using CC for approximately 2" (5 cm), or desired length. At the beginning of the next round, change to MC and continue working in St St until hat measures approximately 9" (23 cm) from cast on, or desired length.

Carefully turn the work inside out while it is still on the circular needle. Holding the needles in a U-shape, divide the sts in half with 42 on each arm of the U. The WS of the hat will be facing outward. Holding the tips of circular needle parallel, use the spare needle to bind off all sts using three-needle bind-off technique. Weave in the ends. Turn hat right side out.

BRAIDED TASSELS (OPTIONAL): For six braids, cut six 20" (51 cm) lengths of each color. For each braid, thread a yarn needle with three strands together (one each of all three colors). Take one stitch at the corner of the hat and pull the yarn halfway through. Remove the needle and adjust the yarn so there are six equal-length strands for braiding. Separate the group into three sets of two colors each. Anchor the hat by pinning it to a board or having a friend hold it, and work a three-strand braid for approximately 4" (10 cm). Tie an overhand knot at the end of the braided section, and trim the ends to 2" (5 cm) long. Make two more braids in this manner on the same corner of the hat. Make three braids for the other corner.

VARIATIONS: Make it striped or make it solid. Use a texture stitch above the rolled edge (remember that you will be knitting in the round and adjust directions for textured stitch patterns accordingly). Include a small intarsia or other color motif at the center front. Add commercially made pompoms or tassels at the corners. Sew on buttons or decorative patches. The possibilities are limited only by your imagination.

chapter five

BY THIS POINT, your knitting skills have been honed along with your skills as a practitioner of mindfulness. With each successive project, you have pushed a little further, whether by introducing a new technique to your knitting or by bringing a new twist to the focus of your mindful meditation exercise. Along the way, each project has invited you to engage purposefully with the work at hand and the work on the needles. Now you will explore how to extend your ever-evolving curiosity to all aspects of your craft and your experience.

skillful knitter

Part of the entire process of relating with our activities purposefully is being open to pushing the comfort zone a little bit. This is the only way we continue to learn. Every knitting project can hold a new jewel of wisdom; hence knitting provides a strong metaphor for our lives. Why does something that seems so simple—a new stitch pattern, or adding a stripe of color—seem so hard and scary? We resist, we are afraid of ruining something we have put so much time into. So what is at the core of this resistance? The beauty of knitting is that we can rip it out and do it over again. I always advise my knitting students to try something new with every project. I ask them to think about something that they think is hard, or that someone told them would be difficult, and find a project that introduces them to this new skill. The obvious secret is to take baby steps—learn how to turn a simple rope cable and choose a project that features that one element rather than decide to try your hand at a multipaneled Aran masterpiece. The former allows you to build solid technical ground, step by step, perhaps culminating in a masterpiece of your own creation. The latter makes you so frustrated you might abandon the project entirely and give up on knitting—what a shame that would be!

fearless knitter

As you continue down your mindful knitter's path, keep a clear sense of what you have learned. Consider it your toolbox of sorts. Then as you contemplate your next project, think about what new tool you would like to put in that toolbox and about what it will teach you from a technical standpoint. What will its inherent lessons be? Since the projects in this book offer a mindful interpretation of very basic items and garments, you can focus on what each new project may hold for you—an opportunity to make a gift for a friend or for yourself. How might it enrich your daily experience? Will it afford you an opportunity to explore your concepts of compassion, obligation, delight, or another feeling? Can you bring to it a mindful focus, or is it a "no-brainer" project that you can use to wind down and practice your integration of tactile sensation?

Alternately, do you have a goal of some kind in your knitting? Do you have that Aran masterpiece in mind, somewhere high up on a pedestal? Or do you want to learn the mechanics of making a sweater? What steps do you need to take to get to that goal? Do you need to practice purling or learn to turn a cable? Do you need to learn how to maneuver double-pointed needles or maybe how to work short rows? Whatever it is, each step up to and including that goal will reveal to you little gems. It might be learning that you hate working with fuzzy mohair because it makes you sneeze. Perhaps you finally figured out how to make a yarn substitution and buy enough of one dye lot to finish the project. Maybe you find great camaraderie at a local yarn shop. Or possibly you find great joy in making wee little hats for the new babies at the hospital and that is all you need to knit for the rest of your knitting career. Whatever you discover, use it to build your confidence, and allow your options for what's next to expand.

While you contemplate these realizations and work through the projects that bring them along the way, remember to be kind to yourself. Don't get carried away in achieving the goal. Remember that the creation of the fabric, stitch by stitch, is a process to be enjoyed. Just as we have goals for ourselves in our lives, we need to remember that every moment is one small step in the process of getting where we are supposed to be. Sometimes we need to rip it out and do it over again—go back to school, leave a relationship, make dinner again because we burned the roast. Remember, it doesn't reflect on who we are, just on what is happening.

In every moment of our lives, we are involved with the continual development of confidence, and the continual expansion of experience. In knitting, as in any skill-building activity, it is no different. Think of it like making soup: it looks like there's no food in the fridge, but with a few basic skills, the proper tools, and a good attitude, some vegetables, water, and other random stuff from the cupboard become a soothing and nourishing meal. Your vegetables and water are your ability to knit and purl, bind off and decrease. Your tools are the yarn, the needles, your mindful focus, your curiosity, and your bravery. Your good attitude is the basic goodness that you can cultivate to bring to all endeavors. And your nourishment will be not only the warm, cuddly sweater you will make, but the gift you give yourself of exploring the process, engaging with it mindfully and expanding your options for what's next. If you choose to make this garment for someone else, the nourishment extends to another, outward into the world.

PROJECT: A SIMPLE SWEATER FOR ALL AGES

If you have completed the basic projects offered thus far, you are so ready for this! This basic sweater, which can be knit up rather quickly in a bulky yarn, offers a wonderful metaphor for bravery in taking on new tasks. As you begin, develop your own contemplation about your purpose for making this sweater—to become a better knitter, because it is really pretty, because you can knit it quickly? Just as there is no wrong answer, there is also no one single answer. Also contemplate how the metaphor of this project might relate to your experience. Here you are given an opportunity to stretch and grow—as a knitter, in your mindfulness skills, and perhaps in some yet undiscovered part of your life. As you create the fabric of this sweater using your now tuned mindful focus, and as you integrate new techniques and new combinations of elements, consider how this theme of expansion and confidence building is relevant for you right now.

It may take a long while to finish this sweater—that's okay. It may be something you put down for six months or more and then return to it like a long-lost friend in a time of crises. That's all right too. As you work through the process, see how making the various parts—back, front, sleeves, finishing—relate to how you move through the situations of your life. Do you see any habitual patterns revealing themselves to you in your knitting? Do you have a recurring thought that may lead to an insight? Whatever arises (even if nothing arises), remember to take joy in the process and pride in the product, but also to stay with the moment and be kind and gentle with yourself.

This cuddly sweater—given here in adult and child sizes—is quick and fun to knit. The pattern builds on your basic knitting skills, combining them with some fun and easy techniques. The thick-and-thin multicolored yarn is a pleasure to touch and to see. This straightforward project will grant you a sense of momentum and pride in your work, reminding you to take joy in the process and to notice how your knitting and the projects you choose act as metaphors for issues in your life. Use your mindful focus to bring to light the most peculiar little things as part of the process. A warm and comforting outerwear garment is a great step onward and outward as a knitter and as a mindful practitioner.

1. Before beginning the knitting of this project, consider spending a few minutes in mindfulness meditation. Once your mind is clear and focused, go to your comfortable knitting spot and pick up your needles.

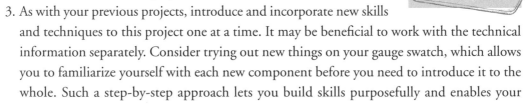

instructions for mindful knitting

2. Enlist your mindful knitting technique, bringing your attention to the formation of the stitches and the physical sensation of the yarn moving through your hands. Be kind to yourself, and take an adventuresome stance on the project.

3. As with your previous projects, introduce and incorporate new skills and techniques to this project one at a time. It may be beneficial to work with the technical information separately. Consider trying out new things on your gauge swatch, which allows you to familiarize yourself with each new component before you need to introduce it to the whole. Such a step-by-step approach lets you build skills purposefully and enables your

mindful knitting session to be focused rather than full of stops and starts. Once you are comfortable with the tools and techniques, return to your mindful focus.

4. What contemplations did you develop at the start of this project? How do they change or evolve as the sweater grows? Consider spending time with each one, and notice how they develop or if they lead your focus away. As always, if you see that your focus has wandered, label your thoughts and return your focus to the formation of the stitch and the physical sensations of the yarn and needles.

5. If you find working with the contemplation too distracting, use your bare attention technique to keep yourself in the present moment, labeling thoughts as they arise and returning your attention to your stitches and your hands. Just as with exploring new knitting techniques, you may wish to integrate one new thing at a time, or explore each new component on its own. If sensations or emotions arise, consider using them as points of contemplation another time.

6. How is this sweater a metaphor for you? Don't actively think about this; just notice what develops both as you are knitting and in your life around the time you are working on this project. Is there something so obvious about the metaphor of this project in your life right now that it is practically whacking you over the head?

7. Make note of your insights and your contemplations in your knitting journal.

8. Be kind to yourself. Ripping out your work is okay and can be very therapeutic, giving you the opportunity to work with your notions of perfection and attachment. Reworking a piece of knitting has a very healing quality to it.

Simple Sweater for a Child

Finished Size: To fit 2 years (4-6 years, 8-10 years)
Chest measurement 30½ (32, 33½)"; (77.5 [81.5, 85] cm)
Total length 16 (18, 20)"; (40.5 [45.5, 51] cm)
Sleeve length 10 (12, 15)"; (25.5 [30.5, 38] cm)

Yarn: Crystal Palace Labrador (100% wool; 90 yards [82 meters]/100 grams): 3 (4, 4) balls main color (MC); 1 ball contrasting solid (CC). Shown in #7266 Tidepool (MC) and #7063 Dutch Blue (CC).

Needles: US 13 (9 mm) circular needle 29" (70 cm) long, or size to give gauge. This project may also be worked on straight needles, but the circular needle will be needed for the front bands.

NOTIONS: Five ½" (1.3 cm) buttons, measuring tape, yarn needle, scissors, stitch holders, crochet hook size J (6 mm), safety pins (optional, for more intuitive buttonhole knitting).

GAUGE: 10 sts and 16 rows = 4" (10 cm) in St St. Check your gauge before you begin.

TECHNIQUES USED: Casting On (page 106), Binding Off (page 106), Stockinette Stitch (page 114), Decreasing (page 108), Three-Needle Bind-Off (page 115), Two-Row Buttonhole (page 91), Picking Up Stitches (page 111), Knitting Flat on Circular Needles (page 107).

Instructions

Back: With MC, loosely cast on 38 (40, 42) sts. Work even in stockinette stitch (St St: knit all sts on RS rows; purl all sts on WS rows) until piece measures 8½ (10½, 11½)" (21.5 [26.5, 29] cm) from cast-on, ending with a WS row.

Armhole shaping: Bind off 3 sts at beginning of next 2 rows—32 (34, 36) sts. Continue to work even in St St until piece measures 15½ (17½, 19½)" (39.5 [44.5, 49.5] cm) from cast-on, ending with a WS row.

Back shaping: Work across 10 sts for all sizes, join 2nd ball of yarn, bind off center 12 (14, 16) sts, work to end—10 sts at each side for shoulders. Working each side separately, work even until piece measures 16 (18, 20)" (40.5 [45.5, 51] cm) from cast-on. Place 10 sts from each shoulder on separate stitch holders.

▲ *See page 60*

DELIBERATE FOCUS GARTER STITCH SCARF *see page 21*

A TRIO OF WASHCLOTHES

see page 30

WARM BLANKET AND HATS

FOR GIVING

see page 42

A SIMPLE SWEATER FOR ALL AGES   *see page 53*

AROMATHERAPY TEA COZY

see page 77

LOTUS SILK PURSE

see page 93

"KATA" FELICITY SCARF   *see page 82*

CABLE CARDIGAN JACKET *see page 84*

ORGANIC BABY LAYETTE *see page 97*

a note on buttonholes

For a woman's or girl's sweater, make buttonholes on right front and sew buttons to left front. For a man's or boy's sweater, make buttonholes on left front and sew buttons to right front. Using two-row, one-stitch buttonhole method, (page 91) make five evenly spaced buttonholes, each 1 st wide, placed on the left or right front as follows: the lowest buttonhole ½" (1.3 cm) up from cast-on, and the remaining four buttonholes 2⅛ (2⅝, 2⅞)" (5.4 [6.7, 7.3] cm) apart for the Simple Sweater for a Child, or 2⅞ (3¼, 3¼, 3¾)" (7.3 [8.3, 8.3, 9.5] cm) apart for the Simple Sweater for an Adult. The highest buttonhole will be at the beginning of the armhole shaping, about ½" (1.3 cm) below the beginning of the V-neck shaping. (Also see "Tip for More Intuitive Knitting: Buttonhole Placement" on page 90.)

Left front: With MC, loosely cast on 19 (20, 21) sts. Work even in St St. If making a boy's sweater, work buttonholes according to "A Note on Buttonholes" above, making each buttonhole in the 3rd st from the end of a RS row. Work even until piece measures 8½ (10½, 11½)" (21.5 [26.5, 29] cm) from cast-on, ending with a WS row.

Armhole shaping: Bind off 3 sts at beginning of the next row, work to end, making last buttonhole for a boy's sweater—16 (17, 18) sts. Work 1 WS row even.

V-neck shaping: (RS) Work to last 2 sts of next RS row, end k2tog—1 st decreased. Work 3 rows even. Repeat the last 4 rows 5 (6, 7) more times—10 sts. Work even if necessary until piece measures 16 (18, 20)" (40.5 [45.5, 51] cm) from cast-on. Place 10 sts for shoulder on stitch holder.

Right front: With MC, loosely cast on 19 (20, 21) sts. Work even in St St. If making a girl's sweater, work buttonholes according to "A Note on Buttonholes" above, making each buttonhole in the 3rd st from the beginning of a RS row. Work even until piece measures 8½ (10½, 11½)" (21.5 [26.5, 29] cm) from cast-on, ending with a RS row, making last buttonhole for a girl's sweater.

Armhole shaping: Bind off 3 sts at beginning of the next row, work to end—16 (17, 18) sts.

V-neck shaping: (RS) Work first 2 sts of row as ssk, work to end—1 st decreased (see page 105). Work 3 rows even. Repeat the last 4 rows 5 (6, 7) more times—10 sts. Work even if necessary until piece measures 16 (18, 20)" (40.5 [45.5, 51] cm) from cast-on. Place 10 sts for shoulder on stitch holder.

Shoulder joining: Using three-needle bind off technique, join shoulders together, right sides facing, carefully matching left front to left back and right front to right back.

Sleeves: With RS facing and MC, using cro-chet hook to assist, pick up 38 (38, 42) sts evenly between armhole notches, with first st picked up at base of notch (notches will be sewn into place later).

Work even in St St for 1" (2.5 cm) or depth of armhole notch, ending with a WS row.

Begin sleeve shaping on the next RS row as follows: K1, ssk, knit to last 3 sts, k2tog, k1—2 sts decreased. Decrease in this manner every six rows 0 (2, 8) times, then every four rows 5 (6, 0) times, then every two rows 4 (0, 0) times—20 (22, 26) sts. Work even in St St until length from armhole pickup is 9 (11, 15)" (23 [28, 38] cm), or 1" (2.5 cm) less than desired length. Change to CC and knit 2 rows. Loosely bind off all sts with CC.

Make a second sleeve the same as the first.

Finishing: Sew sleeve extensions in place at underarm notch. Sew sleeve and side seams, carefully matching MC and CC areas. Weave in the ends.

Bottom edge: With RS facing and CC, beginning at lower left front and using crochet hook to assist, pick up 76 (80, 84) sts along entire bottom edge. Knit one row loosely on WS. Loosely bind off all sts as if to knit on next RS row.

Front band: With RS facing and CC, begin-ning at lower right front and using crochet hook to assist, pick up 82 (92, 102) sts evenly around front opening as follows: 19 (23, 25) sts along right front to beginning of

V-neck shaping, 16 (16, 18) sts along right V-neck to shoulder join, 12 (14, 16) sts across back neck to second shoulder join, 16 (16, 18) sts along left V-neck, 19 (23, 25) sts along left front to bottom edge. Knit one row loosely on WS. Loosely bind off all sts as if to knit on next RS row.

Sew five buttons to right or left front corresponding with buttonhole positions.

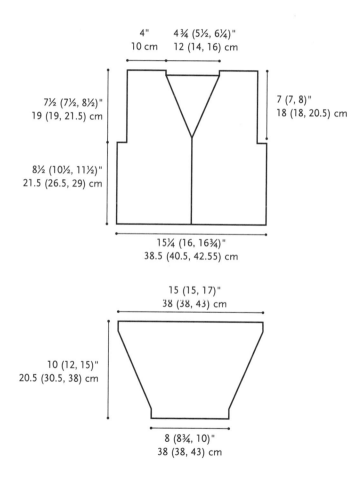

4"
10 cm

4¾ (5½, 6¼)"
12 (14, 16) cm

7½ (7½, 8½)"
19 (19, 21.5) cm

7 (7, 8)"
18 (18, 20.5) cm

8½ (10½, 11½)"
21.5 (26.5, 29) cm

15¼ (16, 16¾)"
38.5 (40.5, 42.55) cm

15 (15, 17)"
38 (38, 43) cm

10 (12, 15)"
20.5 (30.5, 38) cm

8 (8¾, 10)"
38 (38, 43) cm

▲ *Simple Sweater for a Child*

SIMPLE SWEATER FOR AN ADULT

FINISHED SIZE: Unisex: S (M, L, XL):
Chest measurement: 38½ (41½, 46½, 49½)"; (98 [105.5, 118, 125.5] cm)
Total length: 21 (23, 24, 26)"; (53.5 [58.5, 61, 66] cm)
Sleeve length: 16 (17, 18, 18½)"; (40.5 [43, 45.5, 47] cm)

YARN: Crystal Palace Labrador (100% wool; 90 yards [82 meters]/100 grams): 6 (7, 8, 9) balls main color (MC); 1 ball contrasting solid (CC). Shown in #7266 Tidepool (MC) and #5329 Celadon (CC).

NEEDLES: US 13 (9 mm) circular needle 29" (70 cm) long, or size to give gauge. This project may also be worked on straight needles, but the circular needle will be needed for the front bands.

NOTIONS: Five ½" (1.3 cm) buttons, measuring tape, yarn needle, scissors, stitch holders, crochet hook size J (6 mm), safety pins (optional, for more intuitive buttonhole knitting).

GAUGE: 10 sts and 16 rows = 4" (10 cm) in St St. Check your gauge before you begin.

TECHNIQUES USED: Casting On (page 106), Binding Off (page 106), Stockinette Stitch (page 114), Decreasing (page 108), Three-Needle Bind-Off (page 115), Two-Row Buttonhole (page 91), Picking Up Stitches (page 111), Knitting Flat on Circular Needles (page 107).

Instructions:

Back: With MC, loosely cast on 48 (52, 58, 62) sts. Work even in stockinette stitch (St St: knit all sts on RS rows; purl all sts on WS rows) until piece measures 11½ (13, 13, 15)" (29 [33, 33, 38] cm) from cast-on, ending with a WS row.

Armhole shaping: Bind off 4 sts at beginning of next 2 rows—40 (44, 50, 54) sts. Continue to work even in St St until piece measures 20½ (22½, 23½, 25½)" (52 [57, 59.5, 65] cm) from cast-on, ending with a WS row.

Back shaping: Work across 11 (12, 15, 16) sts, join 2nd ball of yarn, bind off center 18 (20, 20, 22) sts, work to end—11 (12, 15, 16) sts at each side for shoulders. Working each side separately, work even until piece measures 21 (23, 24, 26)" (53.5 [58.5, 61, 66] cm) from cast-on. Place 11 (12, 15, 16) sts from each shoulder on separate stitch holders.

Left front: With MC, loosely cast on 24 (26, 30, 32) sts. Work even in St St. If making a man's sweater, work buttonholes according to "A Note on Buttonholes" (page 65), making each buttonhole in the 3rd st from the end of a RS row. Work even until piece measures 11½ (13, 13, 15)" (29 [33, 33, 38] cm) from cast-on, ending with a WS row.

Armhole shaping: Bind off 4 sts at beginning of the next row, work to end, making last buttonhole for a man's sweater—20 (22, 26, 28) sts. Work 1 WS row even.

V-neck shaping: (RS) Work to last 2 sts of next RS row, end k2tog—1 st decreased. Cont in St St, decreasing for V-neck in this manner every other row 0 (1, 1, 3) more time(s), then every 4 rows 8 (8, 9, 8) times—11 (12, 15, 16) sts. Work even if necessary until piece measures 21 (23, 24, 26)" (53.5 [58.5, 61, 66] cm) from cast-on. Place 11 (12, 15, 16) sts for shoulder on stitch holder.

Right front: With MC, loosely cast on 24 (26, 30, 32) sts. Work even in St St. If making a woman's sweater, work buttonholes according to "A Note on Buttonholes" (page 65), making each buttonhole in the 3rd st from the beginning of a RS row. Work even until piece measures 11½ (13, 13, 15)" (29 [33, 33, 38] cm) from cast-on, ending with a RS row, making last buttonhole for a woman's sweater.

Armhole shaping: Bind off 4 sts at beginning of the next row, work to end—20 (22, 26, 28) sts.

V-neck shaping: (RS) Work first 2 sts of row as ssk, work to end—1 st decreased. Cont in St St, decreasing for V-neck in this manner every other row 0 (1, 1, 3) more time(s), then every 4 rows 8 (8, 9, 8) times—11 (12, 15, 16) sts. Work even if necessary until piece measures 21 (23, 24, 26)" (53.5 [58.5, 61, 66] cm) from cast-on. Place 11 (12, 15, 16) sts for shoulder on stitch holder.

Shoulder joining: Using three-needle bind off technique (page 115), join shoulders together, right sides facing, carefully matching left front to left back and right front to right back.

Sleeves: With RS facing and MC, using crochet hook to assist, pick up 48 (50, 56, 56) sts evenly between armhole notches, with first st picked up at base of notch (notches will be sewn into place later).

Work even in St St for 1¾" (4.5 cm) or depth of armhole notch, ending with a WS row. Begin sleeve shaping on the next RS row as follows: K1, ssk, knit to last 3 sts, k2tog, k1—2 sts decreased. Decrease in this manner every six rows 5 (7, 5, 6) more times, then every four rows 5 (3, 7, 6) times—26 (28, 30, 30) sts. Work even in St St until length from armhole pickup is 15 (16, 17, 17½)" (38 [40.5, 43, 44.5] cm), or 1" (2.5 cm) less than desired length. Change to CC and knit 2 rows. Loosely bind off all sts with CC.

Make a second sleeve the same as the first.

Finishing: Sew sleeve extensions in place at underarm notch. Sew sleeve and side seams, carefully matching MC and CC areas. Weave in the ends.

Bottom edge: With RS facing and CC, beginning at lower left front and using crochet hook to assist, pick up 96 (104, 116, 124) sts along entire bottom edge. Knit one row loosely on WS. Loosely bind off all sts as if to knit on next RS row.

Front band: With RS facing and CC, beginning at lower right front and using crochet hook to assist, pick up 120 (130, 134, 146) sts evenly around front opening as follows: 30 (32, 32, 37) sts along right front to beginning of V-neck shaping, 21 (23, 25, 25) sts along right V-neck to shoulder join, 18 (20, 20, 22) sts across back neck to second shoulder join, 21 (23, 25, 25) sts along left V-neck, 30 (32, 32, 37) sts along left front to bottom edge. Knit one row loosely on WS. Loosely bind off all sts as if to knit on next RS row.

Sew five buttons to right or left front corresponding with buttonhole positions.

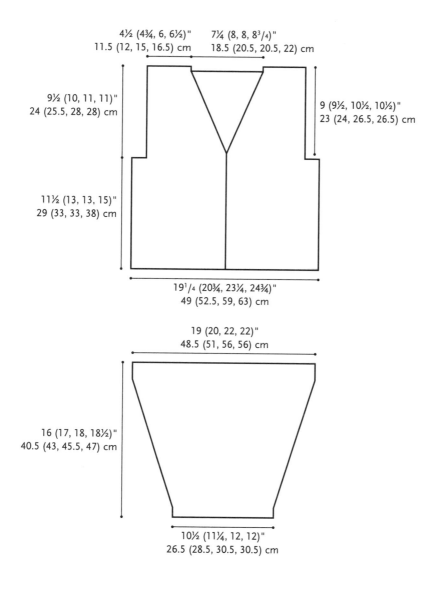

4½ (4¾, 6, 6½)"
11.5 (12, 15, 16.5) cm

7¼ (8, 8, 8³/₄)"
18.5 (20.5, 20.5, 22) cm

9½ (10, 11, 11)"
24 (25.5, 28, 28) cm

9 (9½, 10½, 10½)"
23 (24, 26.5, 26.5) cm

11½ (13, 13, 15)"
29 (33, 33, 38) cm

19¹/₄ (20¾, 23¼, 24¾)"
49 (52.5, 59, 63) cm

19 (20, 22, 22)"
48.5 (51, 56, 56) cm

16 (17, 18, 18½)"
40.5 (43, 45.5, 47) cm

10½ (11¼, 12, 12)"
26.5 (28.5, 30.5, 30.5) cm

▲ *Simple Sweater for an Adult*

part two

MORE MINDFUL KNITTING PROJECTS

chapter six

HERE YOU WILL FIND the mindful knitting supplemental design collection—five additional original knitting projects featuring small quick knits, gift items, and garments. Designed to encourage you to approach your knitting and your actions mindfully, each piece is developed around a contemplative theme—direct experience, giving and receiving, blessings, riches, enrichment, joy, and thankfulness. Each has aspects that will encourage you to continue your journey onward and outward while you simultaneously continue to fine-tune your ability to listen inward. These patterns include steadily advanced knitting techniques, encouraging you to hone your knitting skills and to consider trying something new with every project you undertake. As you browse through these offerings, consider how you, as a mindfulness practitioner and a mindful knitter, can choose to enrich the world whenever possible, through your basic actions and through your love of the craft.

In the Shambhala Buddhist tradition, we reach out to the world by offering a "dedication of merit"—a wish for our individual experiences to continue to move outward from us to benefit others. This prayerlike short chant requests that all beings be free of suffering and enjoy all the brilliance the world has to offer. Some folks use this as a blessing at a meal or simply to reflect upon a pleasant experience; it is also offered after receiving a blessing or teachings from a spiritual teacher.

Think about this idea of radiating the contentment, good wishes, and tranquility you find in your knitting and your mindfulness experiences outward to the world. As you work a project from this collection—or any other project—with attention to mindfulness techniques, you are in fact cultivating awareness and an attitude that benefits yourself and others. As you contemplate this aspect of your work, consider ways to remind yourself of your appreciation of the world and yourself. Consider developing your own dedication of merit, making it relevant to you by composing your own chant or poem to post in your workspace, or to recite when you conclude your knitting sessions. Maybe you can remind yourself of this notion as you complete the finishing work on a piece. You might make a ritual of writing a special inscription for the recipient of your gift as you wrap up an item for giving.

Best wishes on your continued journey. Remember always to be kind to yourself and to extend that gentleness along with your limitless capacity for basic goodness in all aspects of your craft and your life.

the dedication of merit

By this merit, may all obtain omniscience
May it defeat the enemy, wrongdoing
From the stormy waves of birth, old age, sickness, and death
From the ocean of samsara, may I free all beings.

By the confidence of the Golden Sun of the Great East
May the lotus garden of the Rigdens' wisdom bloom
May the dark ignorance of sentient beings be dispelled
May all beings enjoy profound, brilliant glory.

AROMATHERAPY TEA COZY

Healing, generosity, joy, and attention to detail uplift your daily experiences. A delightful gift, this project can be quite a soul soother in both the making and the using. A lavender cozy might help you calm down at the end of a busy day, or present a eucalyptus-filled one to a sick friend with a pot of healing tea. Include a loving wish inside one of the interior pockets and see how long it takes them to find it!

The clever design of this charming cozy includes hidden interior pockets for four hand-stitched herb- or flower-filled sachets. The sachets—which also contain flaxseed to retain heat—can be removed for cleaning or replaced when fragrance fades. Brew a comforting pot of tea and allow the moist, soothing heat from your teapot to release the calming scents of rose and lavender, or the invigorating essence of healing herbs.

The Aromatherapy Tea Cozy is knit in the round in stockinette stitch, allowing for ample mindful knitting and allowing the contemplative knitter to infuse this project with healing, support, or love. Small enough to knit in one or two sessions, this project can simply be enjoyed as the fruit of the comfortable emptiness of a few contemplative knitting sessions.

FINISHED SIZE: 6½" (16.5 cm) tall and 10" (25.5 cm) across, with a 20" (51 cm) circumference.

YARN: Crystal Palace Breeze (100% mercerized cotton; 110 yards [101 meters]/50 grams): 2 skeins main color (MC); 1 skein each or small amounts of cotton scrap yarn in several colors for embroidery. Shown in #27 natural (MC), and #2905 dark green, #6324 light green, #06 dark red, and #2054 pink.

NEEDLES: US 6 (4 mm) circular needle, 16" (40 cm) long, or size to give gauge. US 6 (4 mm) set of 4 or 5 double-pointed needles, or size to give gauge.

NOTIONS: Hand sewing needle, ruler, scissors, measuring tape, yarn needle, stitch markers, crochet hook size F (4 mm).

GAUGE: 24 sts and 32 rows = 4" (10 cm) in St St. Check your gauge before you begin.

SACHET SUPPLIES: Enough cotton muslin, silk, or other sheer, tightly woven fabric for 8 squares, each 3½" x 4½" (9 cm x 11.5 cm), available at fabric or crafts store. For added sentiment, recycle favorite clothing or cherished hankies for cloth.

Sewing thread to coordinate with sachet cloth.

½ cup (approximately 100 grams) aromatic flower petals or herbs. We used dried rosebuds, but you might also consider rosemary, lavender, cinnamon, chamomile, orange peel or blossom, eucalyptus (not preserved), or sage.

¼ cup (approximately 50 grams) flaxseed.

Optional: Aromatherapy essential oil of the flower or scent you have chosen. The last three items are available at your natural food grocer.

TECHNIQUES USED: Casting On (page 106), Joining Work to Knit in the Round (page 111), Stockinette Stitch (page 114), Double-Pointed Needles (page 108), Decreasing (page 108), Three-Needle Bind-Off (page 115). See also "The Better Join" (page 47).

Instructions

With circular needle and MC, loosely cast on 120 sts. Carefully join work into circle, being careful not to twist sts around the needle. Knit the first stitch and place a marker (pm) on the needle to indicate the beginning of the round (rnd). Work even in stockinette stitch (St St; knit all sts every rnd) until piece measures approximately 3½" (9 cm) from the cast-on edge. Purl one rnd to create a fold line. Continue to work even in St St until piece measures 3½" (9 cm), or 3" (7.5 cm) less than desired height from the purled fold line. Knit the next rnd, placing markers as follows: K1, slip existing marker (sl m), k59, pm, k1, pm, k59, pm.

See page 61 ▼

Begin decreasing for top as follows, changing to double-pointed needles when necessary: Decrease round: K1, sl m, ssk, knit to 2 sts before next marker, k2tog, sl m, k1, sl m, ssk, knit to 2 sts before next m, k2tog, sl m—4 sts decreased.

Knit 1 rnd even.

Repeat the last 2 rnds 3 more times—104 sts.

Work the decrease rnd every round 12 times—56 sts.

Fold the work flat, with the sloped decrease lines at each side. Return the sts to the circular needle. Carefully turn the work inside out while it is still on the circular needle. Holding the needles in a U-shape, divide the sts in half with 28 sts on each arm of the U. The WS of the cozy will be facing outward. Holding the tips of circular needle parallel, use a spare double-pointed needle to bind off all sts using three-needle bind-off technique. Weave in the ends. Turn cozy right side out.

Sachets

With sharp scissors, cut eight squares, each 3½" x 4½" (9 cm x 11.5 cm), to make four sachets. This includes ¼" (0.6 cm) seam allowance on all sides, so the finished sachets will measure approximately 3" x 4" (7.5 cm x 10 cm). Place two squares right sides together. Using a running stitch with small, closely spaced stitches, sew your squares beginning about 1" (2.5 cm) from a corner on a long side, stitching toward that corner, continuing around the sachet, and ending about 1" (2.5 cm) from the other corner on the same side to leave a 2" (5 cm) opening (see illustration 1). Don't worry about perfection; just be certain to take stitches small enough to contain the flaxseeds and any other small pieces of your chosen filling. Knot the thread and cut it off. Turn the bag right side out through the opening (see illustration 2).

In a bowl, combine the flowers or herbs and the flaxseed. For a heavier fragrance or to add longevity to the sachets, sprinkle a few drops of aromatherapy oil on the mixture and gently stir. With a spoon, scoop ¼ of the mixture into each sachet through its opening. Sew the opening closed (see illustration

1

2

3). To make each sachet as flat as possible, sew a long running stitch down the center in each direction like a plus sign (see illustration 4). This will help keep the herbs evenly distributed inside the sachet.

Embroidery

If you wish to leave your cozy plain, that's okay. Consider making a light purple cozy and filling it with lavender—that may be enough. If you choose to add embroidered embellishment to your cozy, select a theme that reflects the scent of the sachets, such as the rosebuds shown here. Or embroider your initials, a friend's name, a meaningful word, or a geometric shape. Consider adding other decorative elements such as ribbon roses, buttons, and appliqués of a favorite fabric or wool felt. Use the embroidery diagrams as a guide or inspiration, but don't embroider below the purled fold line because that area will be folded to the inside of the cozy to hold the sachets (unless you want to include a secret or sacred message for the inside).

Sachet Pockets

Turn your cozy inside out and turn up bottom edge along the fold line. Using the MC threaded through a yarn needle, tack the cast-on edge to the inside at four points: once at each side, and once at the center front and back to form four compartments. Slip sachets into the pockets.

Embroidery Stitch Guide

 *Tea Cozy Top Embroidery Motif:*
Lazy Daisy stitch, Backstich, and French Knots

Tea Cozy Bottom Embroidery Motif:
Lazy Daisy stitch, Backstich, and French Knots

Emboidery Techniques

Beginning French Knot

Lazy Daisy

Finished French Knot

Backstitch

 ### sachets

Expand on this idea to create hand-crafted sachets for everyone. A lavender sachet is a traditional gift for a baby's room or bassinet, and lavender under your pillow is believed to bring sweet dreams. Consider taking your embellishment to new levels—words of love on a rose sachet for your beloved, or an understated eucalyptus sachet for you car. Let your imagination go wild. Play around with knitting small rectangular bags with a simple gathered ribbon closure, add a knitted flap closure with a buttonhole, or sew the sachet closed, opening the seam occasionally for cleaning and refreshing with oil. I place sachets inside the cover of my hot water bottle, providing both healing heat and soothing fragrance.

"Kata" Felicity Scarf

In Buddhist culture, the Kata, or Felicity Scarf, is given as an expression of gratitude, a blessing or greeting presented as a sign of deep respect. The literal meaning of Kata is "cloth that binds." Usually made of gossamer woven fabric, a Kata symbolizes a bond between the giver and the recipient. When presented to a spiritual teacher, the Kata is often blessed and returned to the giver as a physical blessing and symbol of connection.

This easy knitted version of the gossamer felicity scarf is made from a simple lace rib. The reversible stitch yields a pattern that looks pleasing on both front and back and is good for learning lace stitches using the yarnover technique. Yarnovers balanced by a compensating double decrease create a delicate scalloplike edge as you knit. Like most knitted lace, this pattern is created by balancing elements across the row, just as we balance the elements in our lives for harmony, and balance our lives with the riches and responsibilities of our relationships. Knit in a luscious soft angora blend yarn in a rich jade color, this scarf is an elegant gift for someone upon whom you may wish to bestow blessings—including yourself.

how to make a yarnover

Bring the yarn forward between the needles, and as you knit the next stitch, wrap the yarn over the top of the right-hand needle to create an extra loop on the needle. On the next row, treat this newly created loop like a regular stitch.

FINISHED SIZE: Approximately 5½" (14 cm) wide and 62" long (157.5 cm).

YARN: Reynolds Devotion (50% angora, 50% nylon; 93 yards [85 meters]/50 grams): 3 skeins #23 jade green.

NEEDLES: US 10 (6 mm), or size to give gauge.

See page 62 ▲

NOTIONS: Scissors, yarn needle, measuring tape.

GAUGE: 13 sts and 13 rows = 3" (7.5 cm) in Razor Shell Lace Rib.
Check your gauge before you begin.

TECHNIQUES USED: Casting On (page 106), Reading Charts (page 112), Binding-Off (page 106).

Instructions

Loosely cast on 25 sts. Beginning with WS Row 1, repeat Rows 1–4 from chart until scarf measures approximately 62" (157.5 cm) long, ending with a RS row. On the next row, loosely bind off all sts. Weave in the ends.

VARIATIONS:

To make a wider scarf, cast on more stitches, making sure that you have a multiple of 6 sts, plus 1, so that the lace pattern will work correctly.

Razor Shell Lace Rib Chart ▲

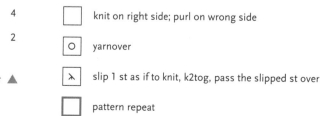

knit on right side; purl on wrong side

O   yarnover

⋌   slip 1 st as if to knit, k2tog, pass the slipped st over

pattern repeat

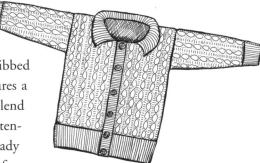

do you have enough left to knit across the row?

To make sure that you have enough yarn to get across the row when joining yarn between skeins, the length of yarn remaining should measure at least five or six times the width of the stitches on the needle. To achieve the longest scarf possible by using all your available yarn, work until the length of yarn remaining is at least six times the width of the stitches on the needle, to ensure that you have enough yarn to bind off.

CABLE CARDIGAN JACKET

The rhythm of knitting this project is a gift of synchronicity to tame the racing mind. A basic cable cardigan with stylish details such as a wide ribbed band and cuffs and smart jacket-like collar, it features a beautiful, hand-painted luscious natural fiber silk-blend yarn. When knitting this jacket, focus on care and intention in every step of the process. The rhythmic, steady turning of the cables creates a metronome effect. This frequency allows for synchronistic, intuitive knitting. Mind, intention, and hand become one, while increasing the knitter's skill and garment vocabulary.

This project is a good second sweater for an ambitious new knitter, and a wonderful contemplative exercise and wardrobe addition for a seasoned knitter. Technical features of this project include a basic rope cable, and increasing the number of stitches between the ribbing and body to create a smooth, pucker-free transition. Through this project, learn to read basic cable symbol charts. After completing this sweater, you will be an expert cabler!

FINISHED SIZE:

Woman's: S (M, L, XL)

Chest measurement: 38½ (41, 46½, 49)"; (98 [104, 118, 124.5] cm)

Total length: 20 (23, 24, 26)"; (51 [58.5, 61, 66] cm)

Sleeve length: 16 (17, 18, 18½)"; (40.5 [43, 45.5, 47] cm)

YARN: Schaefer Yarn Company Marjaana (50% wool, 50% tussah silk; 550 yards [503 meters]/8 ounces [227 grams]): 3 (3, 3, 4) skeins. Shown in Memorable Woman Series IV, Mary Baker Eddy (sage, lilac, wheat, and ice blue combination).

NEEDLES: US 8 (5 mm), or size to give gauge. US 7 (4.5 mm), or one size smaller than main needles.

NOTIONS: Six ½" (1.3 cm) buttons, cable needle, measuring tape, yarn needle, scissors, stitch holders, stitch markers, crochet hook size H (5 mm).

GAUGE: 21 sts and 24 rows = 4" (10 cm) in cable pattern. Check your gauge before you begin.

intuitive knitting tip: cables as a counter

Basic rope cables provide a convenient natural metronome for your knitting. If your project includes a simple four-stitch by four-row rope cable, you can visually keep track of your pattern by the look of the cable. Rather than trying to count rows when you loose your place—which can be very tricky with cables—try turning the cable. You will know right away if you have turned it too soon or too late. If too soon, work two more rows, if too late, you would have had to rip out a couple of rows no matter what. By working with the cables in a more rhythmic fashion, you start to recognize the meter of right- and wrong-side rows—turning the cables on alternate right side rows, and coveting your "rest rows" on the wrong side. See if you can integrate this kind of intuitive looseness into your knitting, and relax into your work.

TECHNIQUES USED: Casting On (page 106), Binding Off (page 106), Textured and Cable Knitting Charts (page 112), Decreasing (page 108), Two-Row One-Stitch Buttonhole (page 91), Three-Needle Bind Off (page 115), Picking Up Stitches (page 111).

STITCHES USED:

Knit One, Purl One Ribbing (worked over an odd number of stitches)

Row 1: *K1, p1; repeat from * to last st, end k1.

Row 2: *P1, k1; repeat from * to last st, end p1.

Repeat these two rows for pattern.

Instructions

With smaller needles, loosely cast on 87 (93, 105, 111) sts. Work in knit 1, purl 1 rib for 3" (7.5 cm), ending with a RS row. Work the next row (WS) as follows, making increases to transition from ribbing to cables: K3, [p1, inc 1 by purling twice into next st, p1, k3] 14 (15, 17, 18) times—101 (108, 122, 129) sts. On the next row (RS), change to larger needles and begin working from cable chart. Repeat rows 1–8 of chart until piece measures 11 (13, 13, 14½)" (28 [33, 33, 37] cm) from cast-on, or desired length to underarm, ending with a WS row.

Armhole shaping: Bind off 8 sts at the beginning of next 2 rows—85 (92, 106, 113) sts. Continue to work even in cable pattern until piece meas 19½ (22½, 23½, 25½)" (49.5 [57, 59.5, 64.5] cm) or 8½ (9½, 10½, 11)" (21.5 [24, 26.5, 28] cm) above armhole shaping.

Back shaping: Work across 22 (25, 31, 34) sts, join second ball of yarn, bind off center 41 (42, 44, 45) sts, work to end—22 (25, 31, 34) sts at each side for shoulders. Working each side separately, work even in pattern until piece measures 20 (23, 24, 26)" (51 [58.5, 61, 66] cm) from cast-on. Note: If there are not enough sts at each side of the neck to work a complete cable crossing, work the cable sts in stockinette stitch (St St:

◀ *See page 63*

knitting the right size and making it fit

The basic shape of this sweater features a drop shoulder and minimal shaping. This allows you to easily alter the length of the body to your perfect fit. To determine the best fit for you, find your favorite sweater or jacket whose fit you absolutely love. Lay it on a flat surface, making sure the side seams and shoulders are folding right at the stitching lines. With a tape measure, measure the distance across from one underarm to the other. Double this number for your ideal circumference. Compare this number to the finished size measurements given in the pattern, and choose the size closest to your ideal.

To determine your perfect length, use the same favorite garment as a guide and measure from the inside of the shoulder (next to the neck opening) down to the very bottom edge. This is your favorite total length. Again, compare the number to the finished size measurements given in the pattern. Perhaps your perfect length and perfect circumference will match up in the same size, but probably not. You will want to knit the size that conforms to your circumference, and customize the length. To make a customization in the length, look at the total length given in the size you have picked. Then refer to the schematic or the diagram of the sweater given at the end of the pattern and note your perfect total length. Next, jot down the armhole depth—or the distance from the beginning of the underarm/armhole shaping to the shoulder. Now subtract the armhole depth from the total length. The resulting number is your personalized length number—the length that *you* will work the body of your sweater before the underarm shaping. For example, the pattern text for the Cable Cardigan Jacket states: "Repeat rows 1–8 of chart until piece measures 11 (13, 13, 14½)" (28 [33, 33, 37] cm) from cast-on, or desired length to underarm, ending with a WS row." If you are making a customization, you will be working your "desired length to underarm" and will replace the numbers given—11 (13, 13, 14½)"—with your personalized length number. The resulting garment will be just right. This method of customizing the length of a sweater works for everyone—men, women, and kids!

knit on RS, purl on WS). Place 22 (25, 31, 34) sts from each shoulder on separate stitch holders.

Right front: With smaller needles, loosely cast on 45 (47, 53, 57) sts. Work in k1, p1 rib for 3" (7.5 cm), ending with a RS row. Work the next row (WS) as follows, making increases to transition from ribbing to cables: K3, [p1, inc 1 by purling twice into next st, p1, k3] 7 (7, 8, 9) times, end k0 (2, 2, 0)—52 (54, 61, 66) sts. On the next row (RS), change to larger needles and establish cable pattern as follows: P0 (2, 2, 0), work cable pattern over next 52 (52, 59, 66) sts. Keeping 0 (2, 2, 0) sts at beginning of RS rows in reverse stockinette stitch (Rev St St: purl on RS, knit on WS), work even in cable pattern on remaining stitches until piece measures 11 (13, 13, 14½)" (28 [33, 33, 37] cm) from cast-on, or desired length to underarm, ending with a RS row.

Armhole shaping: Bind off 8 sts at the beginning of the next WS row—44 (46, 53, 58) sts. Continue to work even in patterns as established until piece measures 17 (20, 21, 23)" (43 [51, 53.5, 58.5] cm) from cast-on, or 3" (7.5 cm) less than desired length, ending with a WS row.

Neck shaping: Bind off 13 (12, 13, 15) sts at beginning of the next RS row, work to end—31 (34, 40, 43) sts. Work one WS row even. Beginning with the next RS row, decrease 1 st at neck edge (using k2tog decrease) every other row 9 times—22 (25, 31, 34) sts. Note: If there are not enough sts at each side of the neck to work a complete cable crossing, work the cable sts in St St. Work even if necessary until front measures 20 (23, 24, 26)" (51 [58.5, 61, 66] cm) from cast-on. Place 22 (25, 31, 34) sts for shoulder stitch holder.

Left front: With smaller needles, loosely cast on 45 (47, 53, 57) sts. Work in k1, p1 rib for 3" (7.5 cm), ending with a RS row. Work the next row (WS) as follows, making increases to transition from ribbing to cables: K0 (2, 2, 0), k3, [p1, inc 1 by purling twice into next st, p1, k3] 7 (7, 8, 9) times—52 (54, 61, 66) sts. On the next row (RS), change to larger needles and establish cable pattern as follows: Work cable pattern over next 52 (52, 59, 66) sts, end p0 (2, 2, 0). Keeping 0 (2, 2, 0) sts at the end of RS rows in Rev St St, work even in cable pattern until piece measures 11 (13, 13, 14½)" (28 [33, 33, 37] cm) from cast-on, or desired length to underarm, ending with a WS row.

Armhole shaping: Bind off 8 sts at the beginning of the next RS row—44 (46, 53, 58) sts. Continue to work even in patterns as established until piece measures 17 (20, 21, 23)" (43 [51, 53.5, 58.5] cm) from cast-on, or 3" (7.5 cm) less than desired length, ending with a RS row.

Neck shaping: Bind off 13 (12, 13, 15) sts at beginning of the next WS row, work to end—31 (34, 40, 43) sts. Beginning with the next RS row, decrease 1 st at neck edge (using k2tog decrease) every other row 9 times—22 (25, 31, 34) sts. Note: If there are not enough sts at each side of the neck to work a complete cable crossing, work the cable sts in St St. Work even if necessary until front measures 20 (23, 24, 26)" (51 [58.5, 61, 66] cm) from cast-on. Place 22 (25, 31, 34) sts for shoulder stitch holder.

Shoulder joining: Using three-needle bind-off technique, join shoulders together, right sides facing, carefully matching left front to left back and right front to right back.

Sleeves: With RS facing and larger needles, using crochet hook to assist if desired, pick up 81 (91, 99, 105) sts evenly between armhole notches, with first st picked up at base of notch (notches will be sewn into place later). Work the next row (WS) as follows, making increases to transition to cables: K3 (5, 3, 3), [p1, inc 1 by purling twice into next st, p1, k3] 13 (14, 16, 17) times, k0 (2, 0, 0)—94 (105, 115, 122) sts.

Working cable pattern from chart over center 94 (101, 115, 122) sts, and keeping 0 (2, 0, 0) sts at each side in Rev St St, work even for 1½" (3.8 cm), ending with a WS row. Beginning on the next RS row, decrease 1 st at each side every 3 rows 11 (7, 5, 4) times, then every other row 15 (24, 30, 33) times—42 (43, 45, 48) sts. Note: If there are not enough sts at each side of the sleeve to work a complete cable crossing, work the cable sts in St St. Work even until sleeve measures 13 (14, 15, 15½)" (33 [35.5, 38, 39.5] cm) from armhole pickup, or 3" (7.5 cm) less than desired length, ending with a RS row. Work the next row (WS) as follows, making decreases to transition to k1, p1 rib: P3 (8, 2, 7), [p1, p2tog, p1, k3] 5 (4, 6, 5) times, p4 (7, 1, 6)—37 (39, 39, 43) sts. Change to smaller needles and work even in k1, p1 rib for 3" (7.5 cm), or desired length of cuff. Loosely bind off all sts in rib.

tip for more intuitive knitting: buttonhole placement

Knit the band that will not have buttonholes first, then mark the button locations with safety pins, either by measuring or "eyeballing it." When you make the band that has buttonholes, compare the band you are knitting to the band with the safety pin markers. When you reach the approximate location of each pin, it's time to make a buttonhole. Continue in this manner until all the buttonholes have been completed.

Make a second sleeve the same as the first.

Finishing: Sew sleeve extensions in place at underarm notch. Sew sleeve and side seams. Weave in the ends.

Left front band: With smaller needles and RS facing, pick up 89 (105, 109, 119) sts evenly along left front, using crochet hook to assist if desired. Work in k1, p1 rib for 8 rows, or until band measures 1¼" (3.2 cm). Loosely bind off all sts in rib.

Right front band: Work as for Left Front Band, making six two-row, one-stitch buttonholes on Rows 4 and 5, the lowest ½" (1.3 cm) up from the lower edge of garment, the highest ½" (1.3 cm) below the beginning of the neck

shaping, and the rest evenly spaced in between, approximately 3¼ (3¾, 4, 4½)" (8.5 [9.5, 10, 11.5] cm) apart.

Securely sew buttons to left front band to correspond to buttonholes on right front band.

Collar: With smaller needles and RS facing, beginning at the right front neck, pick up 103 (105, 109, 111) sts around neck opening as follows: 31 (31, 32, 33) sts along right front neck, 41 (43, 45, 45) sts across back neck, and 31 (31, 32, 33) sts along left front neck. Work even in k1, p1 rib until collar measures 4" (10 cm) or desired length. Loosely bind off all sts.

Two-Row, One-Stitch Buttonhole

Row 1: Work to buttonhole position, bind off 1 st, work to end.

Row 2: On the following row, work to gap created by binding off 1 st in the previous row, cast on 1 st over the gap, work to end.

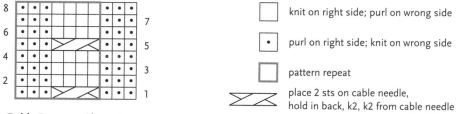

Cable Pattern Chart ▲

knit on right side; purl on wrong side

purl on right side; knit on wrong side

pattern repeat

place 2 sts on cable needle, hold in back, k2, k2 from cable needle

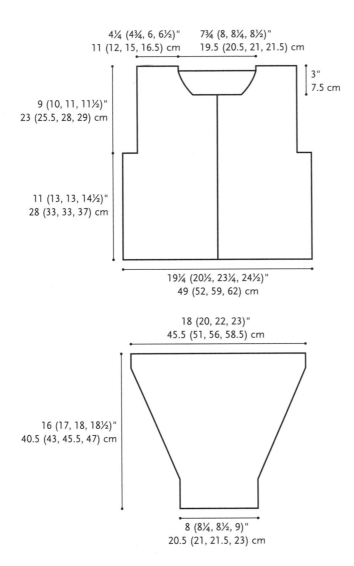

4¼ (4¾, 6, 6½)"
11 (12, 15, 16.5) cm

7¾ (8, 8¼, 8½)"
19.5 (20.5, 21, 21.5) cm

3"
7.5 cm

9 (10, 11, 11½)"
23 (25.5, 28, 29) cm

11 (13, 13, 14½)"
28 (33, 33, 37) cm

19¼ (20½, 23¼, 24½)"
49 (52, 59, 62) cm

18 (20, 22, 23)"
45.5 (51, 56, 58.5) cm

16 (17, 18, 18½)"
40.5 (43, 45.5, 47) cm

8 (8¼, 8½, 9)"
20.5 (21, 21.5, 23) cm

◀ *Cable Cardigan Jacket*

LOTUS SILK PURSE

Many cultures and religions throughout the world and throughout time embrace the lotus as a spiritual symbol with similar meanings and connotations. One of Buddhism's eight auspicious objects, the lotus represents purity, opening of the heart, the inner divine potential, and purification of body, speech, and mind.

In Buddhist symbolism, the red lotus stands for love, passion, and all the qualities of the heart. It is the lotus of Avalokitesvara, the Buddha of compassion. Featuring the motif of a red lotus embellished with bead "jewels," this elegant purse is just the right size for a cell phone and a small wallet, and makes a lovely evening bag. It could hold precious objects—mementos, sacred objects, shrine materials, or prayers. As a gift representing elegance and compassion, it could contain a magical message or a precious object to enhance the life of the recipient.

Knit in luscious shimmering silk, the purse is worked in two pieces, sewn together at the sides and finished off with a matching twisted silk cord. The understated embellishment features semiprecious jewels, yielding a truly exquisite finished piece. The lotus motif is knit using the intarsia method of working a block of color against a background, and is a superb introduction to the technique. The motif is outlined with a simple chain stitch, and the beads are sewn on in a suggested arrangement. Feel free to experiment with the embellishment of this piece, making it truly your own.

FINISHED SIZE: 6½" (16.5 cm) tall and 7½" (19 cm) across at widest point.

YARN: Galler Yarns Jasmine Silk (100% silk; 275 yards [251 meters]/100 grams): 1 skein each of main color (MC) and contrasting color (CC); small amounts of contrast embroidery yarn (shown here in red). Shown in #7050 black (MC), #7010 red (CC).

NEEDLES: US 2 (3 mm), or size to give gauge.

NOTIONS: Scissors, measuring tape, yarn needle, crochet hook size C (3 mm), large-eyed embroidery needle, glass or semi-precious beads for embellishment (shown: five 4mm garnet beads, twenty 4mm peridot beads), beading needle and nylon or silk beading thread.

GAUGE: 7 sts and 9 rows = 1" (2.5 cm) in St St. Check your gauge before you begin.

TECHNIQUES USED: Casting On (page 106), Stockinette Stitch (page 114), Decreasing (page 108), Intarsia (page 110).

Instructions

With MC, loosely CO 31 sts. Work 2 rows St St.

Purse shaping: Inc 1 st at each end of needle every row 8 times—47 sts. Inc 1 st ea end of needle every 3 rows 3 times—53 sts. Work even for 19 rows. On then next row (RS), dec 1 st at each end of needle—51 sts. Dec 1 st at each end of needle every 4 rows 2 times, then dec 1 st at each end of needle every 3 rows 2 times, then dec 1 st at each end of needle every other row 3 times—37 sts; piece measures approximately 6½" (16.5 cm) from cast-on.

Purse flap: Work even for 5 rows. Dec 1 st at each end of needle every other row 3 times, then dec 1 st at each end of needle every row 5 times—21 sts rem. Loosely bind off all sts.

Purse front: Work the first 18 rows as for purse back—51 sts. On the next row (RS), work final increases at each end as established, and at the same time, begin lotus flower motif from chart as follows: Inc 1 st, work until there are 9 sts on right needle, place marker (pm), join CC, work 13 sts from chart, pm, join a second strand of MC, work to end increasing 1 st at end of row—53 sts. Work as established, twisting yarns around each other at color changes to avoid leaving a hole, until Row 9 of chart has been completed. Break off CC, and continue with

▲ *See page 61*

MC only as for purse back, not including the flap—37 sts; piece measures approximately 6½" (16.5 cm) from cast-on. Loosely bind off all sts.

Embroidery: Cut a length of CC approximately 12–14" (30.5– 35.5 cm) long. Separate the yarn into three two-ply strands, as you would for embroidery floss. Using the large-eyed embroidery needle, work chain stitch embroidery around the outside of the lotus motif, maintaining the teardrop shape

▲ *Embroidery with embellishments*

of each leaf. This does not need to be perfect—part of the charm of handmade items is their one-of-a-kind nature. If desired, work additional embroidery and add beads as shown in the embellishment illustration.

Finishing: Weave in the ends on WS. Place purse back and front right sides together, matching shaping. With a yarn needle,

beginning at one end of the bound-off edge of the front, invisibly sew around the side, bottom, and other side of purse, ending at the other end of the bound-off edge of the front. Leave the flap free. If desired, work single crochet across the straight edge at the top of the front opening and around the flap of purse, beginning and ending at one of the side seams. Fasten off and weave in the end.

Twisted Cord Strap: Cut 2 lengths of MC, each approx 4 yards (4 meters) long. Thread both yarns on a yarn needle and draw them through one of the side seam allowances approximately ¼" (0.6 cm) below the top edge of the opening. Bring the ends together so there are four 2-yard (2-meter) strands anchored in the seam allowance in the middle. Place the purse on a table and hold it down with a book or other heavy object. Holding two strands in each hand, twist the strands in the same direction in which the yarn is spun; if the yarn begins to loosen and unravel, you are twisting the wrong direction. Continue to twist until the yarn begins to form kinks. The tighter you twist, the firmer the strap will be. Tie the ends of all four strands together in an overhand knot about 2–3" (5–7.5 cm) from the cut ends, and release. Watch the stored twist energy cause the two groups to twist together, and smooth them out as needed. Pin the knotted end to the seam allowance on the other side and try on the length of the strap. If you want your strap to be shorter, tie another knot farther from the end and trim to that length. Sew the knotted end securely to the other seam allowance.

Closure: If you desire a closure, consider selecting a button or bead that matches either the color or theme of your purse. Make a small loop using single crochet in the center of the bound-off edge of the flap. Determine the placement of your button, and attach it securely to correspond to the loop.

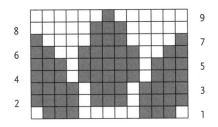

Lotus Chart ▲

☐ With MC, knit on right side; purl on wrong side

■ With CC, knit on right side; purl on wrong side

ORGANIC BABY LAYETTE

Babies' arrivals provide a wonderful
incentive to begin or return to knitting,
allowing us to rediscover its joys. Engaging
in an activity focused on baby helps promote
prenatal bonding, and the meditative benefit of mindful knitting only enhances these qualities. In addition, knitting furnishes a new mom with a
wonderful, sacred connection with her baby. The repetitive
actions of knitting produce a calming effect and have been
shown to lower blood pressure.

This simple-to-knit gift set, designed to welcome and
celebrate a new life, can be completed rather quickly,
allowing the knitter to build confidence, or can easily
fit into the busy day of a new mom. The yarn is a
super-soft, super-fine organic pima cotton made
without chemical pesticides and is amazingly soft as
a cloud—nothing less for baby's delicate skin. Shown in
undyed natural, it is also available in several "colors" that are
cultivated into the seed and grown in shades rather than using dyes. Its natural slubby texture enhances both the use of seed stitch and the organic qualities.

The entire layette set is worked in a large gauge. The sweater is amazingly easy to knit, great
for a newcomer or for intensive mindful knitting sessions. The hat is a super-quick knit and a
useful gift on its own. The blanket is worked in one piece, alternating squares of stockinette and
seed stitch. The knitter of such a delightful gift set can infuse it with blessings and love for the
new child. Think about developing your own unique mindful knitting meditation just for the
new baby as you knit this set of projects—and as you bestow this collection as a gift, consider
it the bestowing of a blessing of love and welcome.

Baby Sweater

Finished Size: To fit 6 months (12 months, 24 months)

Chest measurement: 20 (25, 30)"; (51 [63.5, 76] cm)

Total length: 10 (13, 15)"; (25.5 [33, 38] cm)

Sleeve length: 7 (8, 9½)"; (18 [20.5, 24] cm)

Yarn: Joseph Galler Yarns Inca Cotton (100% organic cotton; 325 yards [297 meters]/8 ounces [227 grams]): 1 (2, 2) skeins Ecru. For combining with other Organic Layette projects, sweater uses approximately 6½ (9½, 13¼) ounces (185 [270, 375] grams).

Needles: US 9 (5.5 mm), or size to give gauge.

Notions: Five ½" (1.3 cm) buttons, measuring tape, yarn needle, scissors, stitch holders, crochet hook size J (6 mm), safety pins (optional, for more intuitive buttonhole knitting).

Gauge: 16 sts and 28 rows = 4" (10 cm) in Seed Stitch. Check your gauge before you begin.

Techniques Used: Casting On (page 106), Binding Off (page 106), Seed Stitch (page 114), Ribbing (page 113), Decreasing (page 108), Three-Needle Bind-Off (page 115), Buttonholes (page 106), Picking Up Stitches (page 111).

Stitches Used:

Seed Stitch (worked over an even number of stitches)

Row 1: *K1, p1; repeat from * to end.

Row 2: *P1, k1; repeat from * to end.

Repeat these 2 rows for pattern.

Seed Stitch (worked over an odd number of stitches)

All Rows: *K1, p1; repeat from * to last st, end k1.

Repeat this row for pattern.

Two-Row, Two-Stitch Buttonhole

Row 1: (WS) Work 2 sts in Seed St pattern, bind off the next 2 sts, work in pattern to end.

Row 2: On the following row, work in pattern to the gap created by binding off sts in the previous row, cast on 2 sts over the gap, work in pattern to end.

Knit One, Purl One Ribbing (worked over an even number of stitches)
All Rows: *K1, p1; repeat from * to end.

Instructions

Loosely cast on 40 (50, 60) sts. Work even in Seed St until piece measures 5 (7, 8)" (12.5 [18, 20.5] cm) from cast-on.

Armhole shaping: Bind off 2 sts at the beginning of the next 2 rows—36 (46, 56) sts. Continue to work even in Seed St until piece measures 9½ (12½, 14½)" (24 [31.5, 37] cm) from cast-on.

Back neck shaping Work across 10 (14, 18) sts, bind off center 16 (18, 20) sts, work to end—10 (14, 18) sts at each side for shoulders. Working each side separately, work even until piece measures 10 (13, 15)" (20.5 [33, 38] cm) from cast-on. Place 10 (14, 18) sts from each shoulder on separate stitch holders.

Right front: Loosely cast on 22 (27, 32) sts. Work even in Seed St until piece measures 5 (7, 8)" (12.5 [18, 20.5] cm) from cast-on.

Armhole shaping: Bind off 2 sts at the beginning of the next row—20 (25, 30) sts. Con-

▲ *See page 64*

tinue to work even in Seed St until piece measures 7½ (10½, 12½)" (19 [26.5, 31.5] cm) from cast-on.

Back neck shaping: At the beginning of the neck edge (opposite side from armhole shaping), bind off 5 (6, 7) sts—15 (19, 23) sts, then decrease 1 st at neck edge every other row 5 times—10 (14, 18) sts. Working each side separately, work even until piece measures 10"(13, 15)" (20.5 [33, 38] cm) from cast-on at each shoulder. Place 10 (14, 18) sts for shoulder on stitch holder.

Left front: Work as for right front, making five two-row, two-stitch buttonholes along center front edge, the lowest ½" (1.3 cm) up from cast-on, and the rest 1⅝ (2⅜, 2⅞)"

(4 [6, 7.5] cm) apart, with the highest buttonhole about ½" (1.3 cm) below beginning of neck shaping. (Also see "Tip for More Intuitive Knitting: Buttonhole Placement" on page 90.)

Shoulder joining: Using three-needle bind-off technique, join shoulders together, right

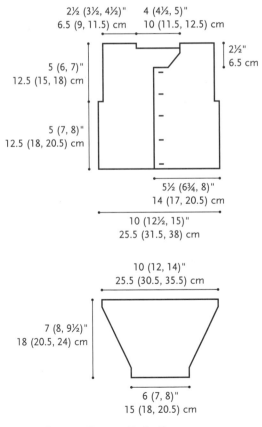

2½ (3½, 4½)"   4 (4½, 5)"
6.5 (9, 11.5) cm   10 (11.5, 12.5) cm

5 (6, 7)"
12.5 (15, 18) cm

2½"
6.5 cm

5 (7, 8)"
12.5 (18, 20.5) cm

5½ (6¾, 8)"
14 (17, 20.5) cm

10 (12½, 15)"
25.5 (31.5, 38) cm

10 (12, 14)"
25.5 (30.5, 35.5) cm

7 (8, 9½)"
18 (20.5, 24) cm

6 (7, 8)"
15 (18, 20.5) cm

▲ *Organic Layette Baby Sweater*

sides facing, carefully matching left front to left back and right front to right back, making sure that the front piece with the buttonholes is the left front. The side of the garment with the three-needle bind-off ridge is the WS of the garment.

Sleeves: With RS facing and using crochet hook to assist, pick up 40 (48, 56) sts evenly between armhole notches, with first st picked up at base of notch (notches will be sewn into place later).

Work even in Seed St for ½" (1.3 cm) or depth of armhole notch. Beginning on the next RS row, decrease 1 st at each side every 6 rows 3 (2, 4) times, then every 4 rows 5 (8, 8) times—24 (28, 32) sts. Work even in Seed St until length from armhole pickup is 7 (8, 9½)" (18 [20.5, 24] cm). Loosely bind off all sts.

Make a second sleeve the same as the first.

Finishing: Sew sleeve extensions in place at underarm notch. Sew sleeve and side seams. Weave in the ends.

Collar: With RS facing and using crochet hook to assist, beginning at the right front neck, pick up 48 (52, 56) sts evenly around neck opening as follows: 16 (17, 18) sts along shaped right front neck edge, 16 (18, 20) sts across back neck, 16 (17, 18) sts along shaped left front neck edge. Work even in k1, p1 rib until collar measures 2½" (6.5 cm) or desired length. Loosely bind off all sts in rib pattern.

Securely sew five buttons to right front corresponding with buttonhole positions.

BABY HAT

FINISHED SIZE: To fit 6 months (12 months, 24 months)
13 (15½, 18)"; 33 (39.5, 45.5 cm) around.

YARN: Joseph Galler Yarns Inca Cotton (100% organic cotton; 325 yards [297 meters]/8 ounces [227 grams]): 1 skein Ecru. For combining with other Organic Layette projects, hat uses approximately 1½ (1¾, 2) ounces (45 [50, 60] grams).

NEEDLES: US 9 (5.5 mm) circular, 16" (40 cm) long, or size to give gauge. US 9 (5.5 mm) set of 4 double-pointed needles, or size to give gauge.

NOTIONS: Measuring tape, yarn needle, scissors, stitch marker (optional).

GAUGE: 16 sts and 28 rows = 4" (10 cm) in Seed Stitch. Check your gauge before you begin.

TECHNIQUES USED: Casting On (page 106), Binding Off (page 106), Seed Stitch (page 114), Decreasing (page 108), Double-Pointed Needles (page 108). See also "The Better Join" (page 47).

STITCHES USED:

Seed Stitch (worked over an even number of stitches):
Rnd 1: *K1, p1; repeat from * to end.
Rnd 2: *P1, k1; repeat from * to end.
Repeat these 2 rounds for pattern.

Instructions

With circular needle, loosely cast on 52 (62, 72) sts. You will need to mark the beginning of your round either by placing a stitch marker on the needle when you complete your cast-on, or by using the cast-on tail to indicate where one round ends and the next begins.

Join the work in a circle, being careful not twist; in other words, make sure that the stitches are not twisting around the needle. If arranged correctly, all the bumps from your cast-on will lie along the same edge of the circular needle, facing in toward the center of the circle. If you choose to do so, mark the beginning of the round and knit the first stitch to close the circle.

Work even in Seed St until hat measures 5" (5, 5½)" (12.5 [12.5, 14] cm) from the cast-on. Rearrange the stitches as evenly as possible on three double-pointed needles; there will not be an equal number of sts on each needle.

Begin decreasing for top of hat as follows:
Decrease Rnd 1: *Work 3 sts in pattern, k2tog; repeat from * to last 2 sts, work last 2

sts in pattern—42 (50, 58) sts.
Decrease Rnd 2: *Work 2 sts in pattern, k2tog; repeat from * to last 2 sts, work last 2 sts in pattern—32 (38, 44) sts.
Decrease Rnd 3: *Work 1 st in pattern, k2tog; repeat from * to last 2 sts, work last 2 sts in pattern—22 (26, 30) sts.
Decrease Rnd 4: *K2tog; repeat from * to end—11 (13, 15) sts.
Decrease Rnd 5: *Work 1 st in pattern, k2tog; repeat from * to last 2 (1, 0) sts, work last 2 (1, 0) sts in pattern—8 (9, 10) sts.

Cut yarn leaving a 12" (30.5 cm) tail. Thread through yarn needle and draw through remaining sts. Fasten securely. Weave in the ends. Fold up cast-on edge desired amount for brim.

sizing a hat for a baby

A hat should be snug—especially for a baby. Choose the circumference that is approximately 1–2" (2.5–5 cm) smaller than the circumference of the baby's head. To make a hat larger or smaller than the sizes given, for every 10 stitches added or subtracted, the circumference of the hat will increase or decrease by 2½" (6.5 cm). Remember, if you are making the hat bigger, you will need more yarn than the amounts stated in this pattern.

BABY BLANKET

FINISHED SIZE: Blanket shown measures 28" (71 cm) square.

YARN: Joseph Galler Yarns Inca Cotton (100% organic cotton; 325 yards [297 meters]/8 ounces [227 grams]): 2 skeins Ecru. For combining with other Organic Layette projects, blanket uses approximately 11½ ounces (325 grams).

NEEDLES: US 9 (5.5 mm) circular, 29" (70 cm) long, or size to give gauge. This project is knit flat on a circular needle, allowing the needle to accommodate the total width of the piece.

NOTIONS: Measuring tape, yarn needle, scissors, stitch markers.

GAUGE: 15 sts and 22 rows = 4" (10 cm) in St St. Check your gauge before you begin.

TECHNIQUES USED: Casting On (page 106), Binding Off (page 106), Seed Stitch (page 114), Knitting Flat on a Circular Needle (page 107), Double-Pointed Needles (page 108).

STITCHES USED:

Seed Stitch (worked over an even number of stitches):

Row 1: *K1, p1; repeat from * to end.
Row 2: *P1, k1; repeat from * to end.
Repeat these 2 rows for pattern.

Instructions

With circular needle, loosely cast on 104 sts. Working flat (back and forth) begin pattern blocks.

Pattern Block 1: Work as follows, beginning with a RS row, and placing markers between the patterns if it will help you to distinguish them more easily:
RS Rows: *Work 14 sts Seed St, p1, work 14 sts St St, p1; repeat from * 2 more times, work 14 sts Seed St.
WS Rows: *Work 14 sts Seed St, k1, work 14 sts St St, k1; repeat from * 2 more times, work 14 sts Seed St.
Work according to Pattern Block 1 for 22 rows, ending with a WS row.

Pattern Block 2: Work as follows, beginning with a RS row:
RS Rows: *Work 14 sts St St, p1, work 14 sts

Seed St, p1; repeat from * 2 more times, work 14 sts St St.

WS Rows: *Work 14 sts St St, k1, work 14 sts Seed St, k1; repeat from * 2 more times, work 14 sts St St.

Work according to Pattern Block 2 for 22 rows, ending with a WS row.

Work 22 rows of Pattern Block 1, followed by 22 rows of Pattern Block 2 twice more—132 rows completed; blanket is 7 squares wide and 6 squares high. Work 22 rows of Pattern Block 1 once more—154 rows completed; blanket is 7 squares wide and 7 squares high. Bind off all sts loosely.

Finishing: Weave in the ends. If desired, work single crochet or trim of your choice around all edges of blanket. Blanket shown features reverse single crochet.

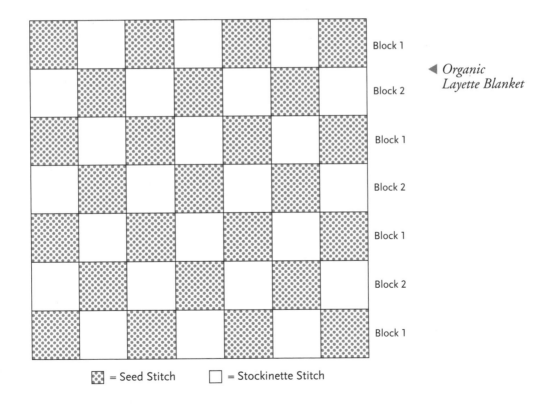

Block 1

Block 2

Block 1

Block 2

Block 1

Block 2

Block 1

◄ *Organic Layette Blanket*

▦ = Seed Stitch   ▢ = Stockinette Stitch

terms and abbreviations

Beg	Beginning		**Meas**	Measures
BO	Bind Off		**MC**	Main Color
CC	Contrast Color		**P**	Purl
CO	Cast On		**PSSO**	Pass Slipped Stitch Over
Cont	Continue		**Pttn**	Pattern
Dec	Decrease		**Rem**	Remaining
DPN	Double-Pointed Needle		**Rep**	Repeat
EOR	Every Other Row		**RH**	Right Hand
Foll	Follows		**RS**	Right Side
Gauge	The number of stitches across and rows up and down in a certain length. Achieving the specified gauge is essential when knitting a pattern.		**Sl**	Slip
			Ssk	Slip, Slip, Knit
			St St	Stockinette Stitch
			St (s)	Stitch (es)
In	Inch		**Tog**	Together
Inc	Increase		**WS**	Wrong Side
K	Knit		**WYIF**	With Yarn in Front
K2Tog	Knit 2 stitches together as one		**YO**	Yarnover
LH	Left Hand			

tips and techniques

Each pattern in this book includes a list of techniques used that may be new to you or to which you might wish to refer. Please consult the list below to find an explanation of the technique in which you are interested.

Binding Off: The technique used to finish off the edge of a knitting fabric, removing it from the needles. Opposite of Casting On. In English knitting terminology, this is referred to as Casting Off. The most common method of Binding Off is to begin by knitting two stitches, then inserting the tip of the left-hand needle into the first stitch knit and lifting it up and over the second stitch knit, then allowing it to drop off the needle. To complete the action, two stitches are required. Once the first stitch is Bound Off, one stitch remains on the right-hand needle. Knit another stitch from the left-hand needle, again giving you two stitches, and repeat the process. If you ever have more than two stitches on the right-hand needle, you have not successfully completed a Bind Off, and need to go back and redo the process with two stitches.

Blocking: Process to even out the tension of stitches and to flatten rolling edges of a knit fabric. Blocking can be done using a steam iron on cool setting, or by washing a garment, shaping it in the desired shape and pinning it in place to dry. Patterned stitches should be blocked *only if absolutely necessary.* Blocking flattens knit stitches and compromises the desired textured effect.

Buttonholes: See "A Note on Buttonholes" (page 65).

Casting On: The technique of putting stitches on the needles to begin knitting a piece of fabric. Many methods of Casting On exist, each giving a unique quality or edge finish. A pattern may call for a particular cast-on to achieve a desired effect or elasticity. Consult a knitting reference book for more information and instructions on the various types of Casting On. The technique recommended for the projects in this book, and for general use, is the Two-Tail Cast-On, also known as the Long Tail or Double Cast-On.

Two-Tail Cast-On—One of the most common methods of Casting On, this method gives a sturdy and neat edge to your work. If you do not know how to complete a Two-Tail Cast-On, please consult an illustrated knitting reference for instruction.

Some tips for Casting On using this method: To measure out a length of yarn for the "tail," a good rule is to measure approximately 1" (2.5 cm) for each stitch you plan to cast on. Then, at the point where you have reached that length, make a slip knot. Place the slipknot on one of the knitting needles and secure it in place. It should be loose enough to slide back and forth but tight enough to stay on the needle if you shake it.

Circular Needles (Circular Knitting): Two short needles attached together by a cord, typically made from plastic. The needles themselves may be made of a variety of materials—aluminum, plastic, wood, or bamboo. Circular needles come in a variety of lengths, most commonly 16, 24, and 29" (40, 60, 70 cm). If you are using them to knit in the round (see below), you should choose a needle with a length slightly less than the circumference of your work.

Knitting in the Round with Circular Needles— The main purpose of circular needles is to allow for knitting in the round, to make a knitted tube. This is done by casting on the required number of stitches, carefully joining the two ends of the cast-on stitches together, and knitting around and around. When knitting circularly, or "in the round," you are only ever working on the "outside" or the right side of the knitted fabric.

Knitting Flat on Circular Needles—Another very helpful use for circular needles is to knit a large piece of fabric back and forth. This may seem counterintuitive at first, but is in fact very efficient and ergonomic. To knit flat using circular needles, cast on the number of stitches given in your pattern, using one of the needles; ignore the other end, letting it flap around while you complete your cast-on. Then begin knitting, pretending as if the two needles were not connected. Work across the row, and then turn your work over, just as you would if you were using straight needles. Again pretending the two needles are not connected, begin the next row. As you work, the knitting itself will hang on the connecting "wire," and you should just skooch it along toward the tip of the left-hand needle, just as you would on a straight needle. A great benefit of knitting flat on circular needles is that the weight of the work is centered, rather than hanging off of one side at the end of a straight needle. You will find this provides great relief to your wrists and shoulders. The other major benefit of this method is that you can knit across a very wide piece of fabric, such as the back of an extra-large sweater or the width of a blanket—items that simply will not fit onto the longest of straight needles.

Decreasing: A method for reducing the number of stitches on your needle. Also a technique for manipulating the shape of a knitted piece, such as making a neck opening rounded or a sleeve smaller at the cuff. The most straightforward and common method of decreasing is to knit (or purl) two stitches together as if they are one. The abbreviation for this action is k2tog (or p2tog). To do this, insert the tip of the right-hand needle into the first two stitches on the left-hand needle, pretending they are one stitch. Then wrap the yarn as usual, and pull one new loop through the two old stitches, letting them both fall off the left-hand needle. Unless otherwise noted, use this method of decreasing for all the projects in this book.

Another method of decreasing is "slip slip knit." The abbreviation for this action is ssk. To do this, slip two stitches, one at a time, from the left hand needle to the right hand needle as if to knit. Then insert the right hand needle into both stitches, behind the left hand needle, and knit the two stitches together. This action is much like k2tog, but you are turning the stitches around on the needle before you knit them together; a k2tog decrease will lean to the right, and a ssk will lean to the left.

Double-Pointed Needles: "DPNs" are short needles with points on both ends that usually come in sets of five. These are used to knit in a circle—or "knitting in the round" (see Circular Needles for more about knitting in the round) when the circumference of your work is too small for a circular needle. In American knitting, knitters typically use four DPNs in their work. It is much easier to get the hang of DPNs if you introduce them into work that has already been established, such as at the top of a hat. When it is time to change to DPNs, hold the first of your four needles in your right hand, letting it become your working right-hand needle. Insert it into the already established work on your existing left-hand needle at the beginning of a round. Start knitting in the established pattern, and work approximately one-third of the stitches. Then let go of the needle. (The tension of the stitches will keep it in place. It is awkward at first, but don't worry.) Pick up the second of your DPNs and repeat this process, and again with the third. When you have worked all the stitches off your former needle, it will become empty; simply set it aside. Now, insert your fourth needle into the next DPN in the circle, which will be the first one you used. Continue around in this fashion. As you empty your left-hand needle, it will become your right-hand needle, and so on. Continue to use your Cast-On tail as a marker to indicate when you have worked all the way around.

Finishing: The assortment of steps and techniques needed to complete a knitting project. Finishing includes things such as blocking, sewing seams, weaving in ends, adding neck finishing and edge treatments, and sewing on buttons. Finishing is usually a love-it or hate-it kind of thing. Many knitters want the sweater or project to be done when the knitting is done, and don't realize the final touches may in some cases take almost as long as the knitting itself. Don't skimp on finishing. You put a lot of time, money, and yourself into your project. Focus your intention on being thorough and proper, and enjoy the details of making your creation as magnificent as it can be. It is good discipline to see the project through to the end with as much purposefulness as you put into it when you started. If you are one of the many knitters who just hate it, consider seeking out an individual who does professional finishing; often one can be found through your local yarn shop. Be prepared to pay a sizable fee for this service, but if you hate it because you find it tedious and time consuming, you will appreciate why they charge as much as they do. If you want to get better at it yourself, and perhaps find the joy in the fine points of the process, see if your local shop or guild offers classes in finishing.

Garter Stitch: The most basic stitch pattern in knitting, garter stitch is created by knitting every row in flat knitting. Both sides look the same. The construction of garter stitch is in fact alternating rows of knit and purl. If you gently pull on the fabric vertically, you can see the row of knit stitches (which look like little Vs) between the ridges of bumpy purl stitch. To create Garter Stitch in the round, you must knit one round, then purl one round.

Gauge: The required number of stitches and rows for a given pattern. You must match the gauge given in the pattern, or else your knitted fabric will not measure to the same dimensions as the pattern, and your project will not be the right size. Nothing is more heartbreaking than completing a project early in your knitting career to find it does not fit or hangs all wrong because you did not take time to properly assess your gauge. Gauge also affects how much yarn will be used.

Before you begin any project, knit a gauge swatch or sample piece. This will enable you to measure the size of your stitches and to practice the stitches used in the project. Most patterns give a gauge in terms of a 4" (10 cm) square piece of knitting. Begin using the needle size recommended in your project. This is the *recommended* needle size—a starting point. When you cast on for your swatch, cast on at least 4 stitches more than the number you wish to measure. In other words, if your desired gauge is measured over 20 stitches, cast on 24 or more, and work it for more than 4" in length. This is for several reasons. First, the larger your swatch, the more accurately it can be measured. Second, it is best to measure gauge over a central section of the fabric unobscured by selvage edges, the Cast–On, and the needles. If you simply cast on 20 stitches and check to see if it is 4" across, you will be doing yourself and your project an injustice.

Use a tape measure, "Knit Check" tool, or ruler to count the number of stitches you are knitting in the given width (i.e., over 4 inches [10 cm]). If you do not have enough stitches, go to a smaller needle; if you have too many, go to a bigger needle. Keep moving your needle size up or down as needed until you get the stitch count dead on. Remember, it won't take you any longer to knit your project on a smaller needle—if you're getting proper gauge, your stitches are the exact same size as the recommended needle size!

Intarsia: Technique for knitting blocks of color using a strand of each color for each block worked. Rather than having many colors attached to lots of different balls of yarn, each color is often wound onto a bobbin and left to hang off the back of the piece until you work your way back to it and need it again. Unlike stranded knitting, such as you would see in a Nordic-style sweater, intarsia blocks are worked without carrying yarns behind the work. Rather, the yarn for each color used is isolated, kept to the confines of its particular color block. When working an intarsia block of color, it is important to twist the two yarns together, "locking" them when you change from one color to the next so as not to knit a slit into your piece. For more information on intarsia and color knitting in general, please consult a well-illustrated knitting reference book.

Joining Work to Knit in the Round: When you join your work into a circle to knit in the round, it is very important to make sure that the stitches are not twisting around the needle. Patterns will say, "Join, being careful not to twist." To see easily whether your stitches are lined up straight, place the needles flat on a table and manipulate the work so that the straight edge of stitches created by your cast-on points in toward the center of the circle. Continuing to use the table as a "third hand" if desired, pick up the needle with the yarn attached to ball coming off it (i.e. the very last stitch you cast-on) in your right hand. Insert the right-hand needle into the first stitch on the left-hand needle and work the first stitch with the yarn that is coming from the right side. This will join the piece into a circle. Then simply begin knitting around and around. Use the Cast-On tail as a marker to indicate when you have come all the way around the work and are starting the next round. For a tip on how to better join your work in the round, see "The Better Join" (page 47).

Picking Up Stitches: This is usually done to create an edge finish or to knit a new part of the project, such as a sleeve, out from a piece of existing fabric. In the patterns in this book, stitches for the sleeves are picked up at the armhole edge and knit down to the cuff, rather than knitting them separately and sewing them on later. To pick up stitches more neatly and evenly, consider using a crochet hook to help you. With the right side of the fabric facing you, lay down a strand of yarn behind the fabric. Always pick up stitches toward your ball of yarn. Find the location where you will begin picking up stitches, plunge the crochet hook through, and pull through a loop made from the yarn stranding behind. Place this on the right-hand needle. Repeat until you have the number of stitches you need.

To intuitively pick up stitches, note how many stitches you need to pick up. Mentally divide this number into 4, and note where four quadrants will be on your piece. For example, when picking up stitches for a sleeve, if you begin at the underarm, the shoulder seam will be halfway.

Therefore, halfway to the shoulder seam, you should have a quarter of the stitches already picked up. If you need to make up for extra stitches, place them close to the underarm. Because there are typically more rows to the inch than stitches to the inch, a good rhythm when picking up stitches along a side edge is to pick up into two rows, skip a row, and then repeat. If they don't look right, they are easily pulled out and retried. The practice is helpful to hone your skill.

Reading Charts: Knitting charts are a universal visual "language" for knitting. They are read as if looking at the right side of knitted fabric. When knitting flat, charts are read back and forth, just like the construction of the fabric. Begin in the lower right-hand corner on right-side rows and read from right to left. For wrong-side rows, read from left to right, zigzagging as you go. If knitting in the round, always start at the right-hand side and work right to left, working the symbols exactly as shown.

Although it may feel like learning a new language, becoming comfortable with symbol charts is a wonderful way to become a more intuitive knitter. Once you are familiar with them, the symbols actually look like the completed pattern. This visual language can liberate you from written instructions and long strings of abbreviations such as "P2, K6, P2, C4B, P2, C5F, LT," and other such maddening left-brain fodder. You can begin to interact with the work in such a way that your knitting will actually tell you what to do next. Furthermore, knitting symbols are an international language. Once you are familiar with the basic symbols, you can knit fun and truly exciting projects from any foreign book or magazine that utilizes them.

Textured and Cable Knitting Charts—Charts represent the right side of the knitted fabric. Therefore, a stitch that should be purled on the wrong side will be shown as a knit stitch. A blank square indicates a knit stitch on the right side, a purl stitch on the wrong side, and a square with a dot indicates a purl stitch on the right side, and a knit stitch on the wrong side. A symbol key accompanies each knitting chart. If you are working a project with cables, written instructions will accompany the unique symbol for making the cable. A chart for lace will use the symbols specific to the increasing and decreasing methods for lace. You should work the action indicated (i.e., turn the cable or work a decrease as instructed) at the location where the symbol is shown.

Color Knitting Charts—Charts showing patterns for more than one color are read in much the same manner as texture charts, representing right side of the knitted fabric. A symbol key accompanies the chart, giving you details on which color or symbol used in the chart represents the main color (MC) and the contrast colors (CC). For projects in this book, if multiple contrast color are used, they will be referred to as contrast color 1 (CC1), contrast color 2 (CC2), and so on. The number of squares shown in a certain color indicates the number of stitches you are to work in that color. Carrying a second color behind your knitting to use later is called stranding. Always strand your colors loosely or your tension will be effected. If you strand too tightly, the stitches made with that yarn will recess behind the main color and may disappear entirely.

Reading a Knitting Pattern: See "Reading a Knitting Pattern" (page 22).

Ribbing: Most familiar as the classic edge treatment traditionally found on sweaters, Ribbing creates a very stretchy, elastic fabric and is generally made up of alternating knit and purl stitches stacked on top of one another. The two most common forms of ribbing are knit one, purl one ribbing (1/1 ribbing) and knit two, purl two ribbing (2/2 ribbing). Instruction for knitting these two forms of ribbing are as follows:

Knit One, Purl One Ribbing (to be worked over an odd number of stitches):
Row 1: (RS) Knit 1, * purl 1, knit 1, repeat from * to end of row.
Row 2: (WS) Purl 1, *knit 1, purl 1, repeat from * to end of row.
Repeat rows 1 and 2 for desired length or as instructed in your pattern.

Knit Two, Purl Two Ribbing (to be worked over a multiple of 4 stitches plus 2 extra):
Row 1: (RS) Knit 2, * purl 2, knit 2, repeat from * to end of row.
Row 2: (WS) Purl 2, * knit 2, purl 2, repeat from * to end of row.
Repeat rows 1 and 2 for desired length or as instructed in your pattern.

When you see an instruction like this for the multiple of stitches needed for a stitch pattern, think of it much like when a cookbook instructs you to use 2 cups of flour plus a tablespoon. In other words, for this stitch pattern (2/2 ribbing), you must first determine what your multiple of 4 is—any number divisible 8, 12, 16, 20, 24, and so on. Then, after you have cast on that number of stitches, add two more at the end, so that the pattern will come out balanced. If it's not making sense, don't think about it too hard; just have faith it will work.

Seed Stitch: A basic and very texturally appealing knit and purl stitch combination. Easy to knit, seed stitch is constructed of a little checkerboard of knit and purl stitches. If you feel bored with basic garter and stockinette stitch projects, seed stitch is a great way to enhance your projects with some interest without increasing the difficulty or adding elements that might be distracting to your focus. Seed stitch is identical on the front and back (right and wrong sides) and is a good pick for any project you want to be reversible. Instructions for seed stitch are as follows:

Seed Stitch (worked over an even number of stitches):
Row 1: (RS) * Knit 1, purl 1, repeat from * to end of row.
Row 2: (WS) * Purl 1, knit 1, repeat from * to end of row.
Repeat rows one and two.

Stockinette Stitch: The stitch most people think of when they think of knitting, stockinette stitch features the smooth, knit stitch on the outside (right side) and the bumpy purl stitch on the inside (wrong side). It is created by stacking rows of the same stitch on top of themselves by alternating rows of knit and purl. This alternation gives stockinette stitch a nice rhythmic quality. Use of a textured or hand-painted/multicolored yarn greatly enhances the basic nature of stockinette stitch. Instructions for working stockinette stitch are as follows:

Stockinette Stitch (worked over any number of stitches):
Row 1: (RS) Knit across the row.
Row 2: (WS) Purl across the row.
Repeat rows 1 and 2.

Tail (Cast-On Tail) as Marker: See "Tip for Intuitive Knitting: Right Side/Wrong Side and the Telltale Tail" (page 33).

Three-Needle Bind-Off Technique: A join that produces what looks like a perfect seam and is performed using three needles—two that are holding the live stitches of the pieces to be joined, and a third used for working the bind-off. The basic action is almost identical to that of a standard bind-off. This is a wonderful way to join two pieces of knitting in place of sewing a seam, especially effective when used to join shoulders. The method is also referred to as binding off two pieces together.

To perform this technique, place stitches that may be on hold onto two needles, so that right sides of the fabric face each other and the tips of both needles point in the same direction. If you are joining shoulders, make sure you carefully match left shoulder to left shoulder and right to right. Hold these two needles parallel to each other in your left hand to act as the left-hand needle. Using a third needle as the right-hand needle, insert this right-hand needle through the first stitch on the front needle and the first stitch on the back needle in your left hand. Knit the two stitches together as one and slide them both off their respective needles. Repeat, creating a second stitch on the right-hand needle. Then perform the first bind-off by slipping the first stitch worked over the second stitch worked and off the needle. Repeat the process until all stitches are bound off. Cut the yarn, leaving a 6"–10" (15–25 cm) tail and draw the tail through the final remaining loop. Weave in the end.

If you are having a hard time visualizing this process, give it a try. If you are still not getting it, please consult a well-illustrated knitting reference book or ask a knitting friend for a demo.

Weaving in the Ends: A crucial part of finishing your work (see Finishing, above). Ends, just like knots, have a nasty little tendency to wiggle their way to the front of your work, especially if you have ends front and center—and it seems like there are always ends to weave in at the front and center of a sweater. To minimize the number of ends to weave into your fabric, always try to join a new yarn at the beginning of a row (see "Do You Have Enough Left to Knit across the Row?" on page 84). To make weaving ends easier, try to leave yarn tails that are at least 8" (20 cm) long. When weaving in an end on a seam, thread the yarn through a yarn needle and sew up the same path as your seam for about an inch. Then double over the top and trace your path back about an inch. This secures the yarn very well and allows you to cut the yarn flush against the fabric. If you have to weave in an end in the middle of your knitted fabric, work the trajectory of the yarn needle on a diagonal, making sure the yarn you are weaving is not visible from the right side. Then double back and trace your path back to where you started. Again, this allows you to cut the end flush with the fabric. Working on a diagonal minimizes the amount of tug on the end, making it more likely to stay put and not wiggle its way out.

Bare Attention: An intense form of paying attention, placing your attention on what is occurring in the moment without embellishment or interpretation.

Basic Goodness: A quality present in every being, every experience, and every moment, embodying the capacity within all things and all situations to wake us up to the preciousness of experience and the power of the present moment. A very compassionate concept, acknowledgment of this capacity for this goodness in ourselves allows us to recognize it in others.

Contemplative: Contemplative or "mindful" activities are those that create a space which allows your mind to exist fully in the present moment. For some people this may be an activity such as prayer, for others it is gardening, yoga, or meditation. The traditional definition of "contemplative" is to be thoughtful and to engage in prayer.

Dharma: The teachings of the Buddha.

Enlightened Society: An idea of a world built upon generosity and kindness where everyone mindfully contributes to the support and well-being of all. Inherent in this vision of society is a sense of social responsibility and compassion as well as the fundamental acknowledgment of human dignity, preciousness of experience, and recognition of the goodness inherent in all beings.

Kagyü: Literally "oral lineage" or the line of spoken transmission. One of the four main schools of Tibetan Buddhism; the Kagyü Lineage is known for its strong emphasis on meditation practice; this lineage traces its origin back to Shakyamuni Buddha.

Mindfulness: Engaging in moment-to-moment awareness, allowing yourself to be aware of what is happening in your mind and in your surroundings without judgment or interpretation —simply as an observer.

Nowness: The skill of bringing your mind and your actions into the present moment. Completely experiencing what is happening as it happens.

Nyingma: The oldest of the four schools of Tibetan Buddhism.

Rigdon: 1. Imperial rulers of Shambhala.
2. Enlightened awareness.

Rinpoche: Title of honor and respect used in reference to a Tibetan Buddhist teacher.

Samsara: Cycle of birth, suffering, death, and rebirth.

Sangha: A community of like-minded people with common vision. Traditionally a community of spiritual practitioners.

Shamatha: Literally means "peacefulness." A basic form of mindfulness meditation, common to most schools of Buddhism, which often uses the flow of breath as tool of focus.

Shambhala: 1. An ancient kingdom said to have existed high in the Tibetan plateau centuries ago—the basis of the legend of Shangri-La. Shambhala is believed to have been a culture of fearlessness, dignity, and compassion.

2. A tradition of teachings based on a viewpoint that there is a natural radiance and brilliance in the world, the source of which is the innate wakefulness and dignity of human beings.

Warriorship: The qualities of dignity and abundance that are always available to us through our connection with awareness of the present moment and the notion of basic goodness.

bibliography and further reading

Beck, Charlotte Joko. *Everyday Zen.* New York: Harper San Francisco, 1989.

Chödrön, Pema. *The Places that Scare You.* Boston: Shambhala Publications, 2002.

———. *Start Where You Are.* Boston: Shambhala Publications, 2001.

———. *When Things Fall Apart.* Boston: Shambhala, 2001.

———. *The Wisdom of No Escape.* Boston: Shambhala Publications, 1991.

Editors of Vogue Knitting. *Vogue Knitting: The Ultimate Knitting Book.* New York: Sixth and Spring Books, 2002.

Hyde-Chambers, Frederick. *Tibetan Folk Tales.* Boston: Shambhala Publications, 1981.

Mipham, Sakyong. *Turning the Mind into an Ally.* New York: Riverhead, 2003.

Trungpa, Chögyam. *Cutting through Spiritual Materialism.* Boston: Shambhala Publications, 1973.

———. *Great Eastern Sun: The Wisdom of Shambhala.* Boston: Shambhala Publications, 1999.

———. *Journey without Goal.* Boston: Shambhala Publications, 1981.

———. *The Lion's Roar.* Boston: Shambhala Publications, 1992.

———. *Shambhala: The Sacred Path of the Warrior.* Boston: Shambhala Publications, 1984.

Walker, Barbara. *A Treasury of Knitting Patterns.* New York: Scribners, 1968.

materials sources

Project kits and Tara's original design patterns are available from:
Tara Handknitting Designs
PO Box 573
Boulder, CO 80306-0573
www.tarahandknitting.com

suppliers

Many heartfelt thanks are extended to the manufactures and distributors of the fine yarns and notions shown in this book.

Artful Yarns
Distributed by JCA, Inc.
Project: Deliberate Focus Garter Stitch Scarf

Crystal Palace Yarns
2320 Bissel Avenue
Redmond, CA 94804
(800) 666-7455
www.straw.com
Projects: A Trio of Washcloths, Simple Sweater for a Child, Simple Sweater for an Adult, Aromatherapy Tea Cozy

JCA, Inc.
Distributor of Reynolds Yarn and Artful Yarns
35 Scales Lane
Townsend, MA 01469
(800) 225-6340

JHB International
1955 South Quince Street
PO Box 22395
Denver, CO 80222
(800) 525-9007
orders@buttons.com
www.buttons.com
Buttons shown in this book were provided by JHB International.

Joseph Galler Yarns
5 Mercury Avenue
Monroe, NY 10950-9736
(800) 836-3314
Projects: Organic Baby Layette Sweater,
Silk Lotus Purse
For more information about organic products and yarns, see below.

Mission Falls
Distributed in the U.S. by Unique Kolors
1428 Oak Lane
Downingtown, PA 19335
(800) 25-2DYE4
www.missionfalls.com
Projects: Warm Blanket and Hat for Giving

Schaefer Yarn Company
3514 Kelly's Corners Road
Interlaken, NY 14847
(800) 367-9276 (800-FOR-YARN)
www.schaeferyarn.com
Project: Cable Cardigan Jacket

Reynolds Yarns
Distributed by JCA, Inc.
Project: "Kata" Felicity Scarf

local yarn shops

Keep the local knitting community in your area flourishing by supporting your local yarn and crafts shops. These independent retailers are often the heart and hub of knitting groups, friendships, and support networks. To find a local yarn store, visit one of the internet sites listed here, or run a search through your favorite internet search engine for "your town + yarn shop." Yarn shops come and go, so check your current phone book for up-to-date contact information.

Knitter's Magazine Shopfinder: www.knittingunivers.com/athena.shopfinder.taf

Interweave Press Traveling Knitter's Guide: www.interweave.com/travelingknitters.html

WoolWorks: www.woolworks.org/stores.html

About.com's knitting resources: www.knitting.about.com/cs/yarnshopreviews

organic yarns and products

For information about the impact of choosing to buy organic and about U.S. Organic standards, production, and products, visit the National Organic Program at www.arms.usda.gov/nop and the Organic Trade Association at www.ota.com.

shambhala resources

Shambhala Training International

Shambhala Training is the secular study and practice of Shambhala warriorship—the tradition of human bravery and leadership. The Shambhala warrior's path shows us how to address the challenges of daily life and the modern world as opportunities for contemplative practice and social action. In a series of weekend meditation workshops for both beginning and experienced meditators, Shambhala Training uses a simple and profound technique of mindfulness meditation that cultivates mindfulness and awareness. By utilizing such a mindfulness meditation technique to look directly at our own experiences, we are able to connect with the basic dignity that exists in all beings. More information about Shambhala Training can be found at www.shambhala.org.

Shambhala Buddhism

For more information about Shambhala Buddhism and Shambhala study, practice, and retreat centers, visit these websites or contact Shambhala International through the address below:
www.shambhala.org
www.mipham.com

Shambhala International
1084 Tower Road
Halifax, Nova Scotia
Canada, B3H 2Y5

online knitting resources

Check in with the global knitting community online—surf these sites to see what other wired knitters are up to or to browse up-to-the-minute knitting 'zines. More sites than those listed here can be found through an internet search engine.

www.knitty.com—online knitting magazine.

www.knitnet.com—online knitter's resource and magazine.

www.woolworks.org—informational site with directories, chat, patterns, and more.

www.tkga.com—the Knitting Guild Association, organizing group for the Knitting Guild of America. Find resources here on how to start or join a guild.

charity knitting

Many groups have been formed to support charitable giving and knitting-to-help worldwide, a wonderful way to help the world and have your knitting make a difference. Well-maintained lists of charitable knitting websites can also be found at: Woolworks (www.woolworks.org/charity.html) and KnitLit Project (www.knitlit.com). Following is just a sample listing of these groups, and most of these sites include advice and encouragement on how to start your own charitable knitting group.

Afghans for Afghans

www.afghansforafghans.org

This humanitarian and educational project provides hand-crafted blankets and garments to the beleaguered people of Afghanistan.

Caps for Kids

www.geocities.com/Heartland/Hills/3272/capsforkids.html

Supported by yarn shops around the U.S., this foundation collects hand-crafted caps for underprivileged kids. Caps are collected by participating shops and are then distributed in the community through local nonprofit agencies. Check the website to see if there is a participating shop in your area.

Chemo Caps

www.chemocaps.com

This group knits caps for cancer patients in hospital oncology units and hospice programs, so that patients who loose their hair have a soft hand-knit hat to call their own, comforting hearts and souls.

Project Linus

www.projectlinus.org

A volunteer group, their mission is to provide love, warmth, and support to seriously ill, traumatized, and needy children through the gift of new hand-crafted blankets and afghans.

Special Knitting Forces

www.specialknittingforces.org

Through donation of hand-knit items, this organization brings comfort to civilians during wartime—especially babies, children, and families.

Warm Up America

www.warmupamerica.com

This foundation distributes hand-crafted blankets and afghans to individuals and families in need across the U.S. The group maintains a list of charitable and community service agencies providing assistance to the homeless, battered women's shelters, and people in need.

knitting groups

Ask at your local yarn shop for information on local knitting groups and guilds. Consider starting a group in your area by posting a notice at a community center, yarn shop, church, or coffee shop. Many already established groups and guilds can be located through a simple internet search engine using the key words "knitting group + your town." The Knitting Guild Association (www.tkga.com) may also be able to tell you if a formal guild exists near you.

starting a mindful knitting group

If you have found the mindful knitting approach helpful as a contemplative practice, consider forming a mindful knitting group in your area. In establishing this kind of sangha, you will be able to share and explore your own views about how knitting is fulfilling and both find and provide support for other like-minded knitters. You could simply meet as a social group with similar interests, or take a more formal approach by using the themes and instructions in this book to further explore using your cherished handwork as a forum for working with the world mindfully. Gather a few friends or post a notice at your place of worship, meditation center, local yarn shop, or favorite coffee shop. Consider discussing how your knitting sangha can share its inspiration and compassion—perhaps by teaching others to knit or by starting a charity knitting project. Remember, your ability to inspire and share the elements of basic goodness is limited only by you.